chef's salad . bill jones

Have fun with the recipes!
Bill Jones

chef's salad . bill jones

whitecap

Edited by Elaine Jones
Proofread by Lesley Cameron
Cover and interior design by Roberta Batchelor
Food photographs by Andrei Fedorov
Food styling by Bill Jones

Printed and bound in Canada

National Library of Canada Cataloguing in Publication Data

Jones, W. A. (William Allen), 1959-
   Chef's salad: green, vegetable, pasta, bean, seafood, potato/ Bill Jones; Photographer, Andrei Fedorov; Foreword, James Barber.

   Includes index.
   ISBN 1-55285-419-1

   1. Salads . I. Title.
TX807.J66 2003   641.8'3   C2003-910432-X

The publisher acknowledges the support of the Canada Council for the Arts and the Cultural Services Branch of the Government of British Columbia for our publishing program. We acknowledge the financial support of the Government of Canada through the Book Publishing Industry Development Program for our publishing activities.

Contents

DEDICATION

This book is dedicated to all of the hardworking people who make great food possible. Farmers, producers, purveyors, cooks and chefs all deserve our gratitude and respect.

Acknowledgements

Books are like a garden, first the seed of an idea must be planted. Then the plans must be protected and nourished to maturity. Holding a newly minted book hot off the press is like plucking a carrot from fertile soil and savoring the efforts of all your hard work and perseverance. On the home front, I would like to thank Lynn, my wife and self-proclaimed gardening addict. Without her support, our dream of a farm and country lifestyle would have disappeared faster than a lettuce bed attacked by slugs. Special thanks go to my father-in-law Ken Wilkinson for his support and tireless contribution as our chief unpaid laborer. As P.T. Barnum said — "there's one born every minute." I am forever grateful to my parents, Bill and Joan Jones, for their love and encouragement of a son who has often taken the road less traveled (sometimes there weren't even roads).

The staff at Whitecap should stand up and take a bow for producing and marketing a strong range of Canadian cookbooks. Publisher Robert McCullough started the project off on a good note with enthusiasm for the proposal and passed the baton to Robin Rivers and her excellent production team. Elaine Jones did the bulk of the editorial work on the manuscript and deserves credit for making the text elegant and user-friendly. Sophie Hunter worked very hard on all promotional aspects and brought welcome enthusiasm to the project. Thanks to all the great people at Whitecap.

The wonderful photographs are courtesy of Andrei Fedorov. He is a very talented artist who, along with his wife Doris, invited me into their home and allowed me to take over the kitchen for our photo shoot. His delightful daughters Kristina, and Sofi, contributed to making the sessions fun, creative and always entertaining.

And last but not least, a heartfelt thank you to all the people who have generously made time to educate me on the world of food. Friends and mentors like author James Barber, food activist Herb Barbolet of FarmFolk.CityFolk and proprietor Sinclair Philip of Sooke Harbour House have encouraged me along the garden pathway. Chefs like Anton Mosimann, Michael Stadlander and Edward Tuson have inspired me to create dishes based on the simple organic beauty of food and confirmed that passion, commitment and an unwillingness to compromise principles are at the heart of all great chefs.

Bill Jones
The Cowichan Valley
Vancouver Island, BC.
Winter, 2003

Foreword

Salads in North America have always had a hard time being recognized as food. For years and years there was very little more than lettuce, and such lettuce at that — dreary iceberg, coiled tight in a ball like old wrapping paper, no color, no character, no redeeming features at all. No wonder kids didn't like it, no wonder the cookbooks concocted such desperate recipes for it. Canned orange segments, marshmallows, melonballs, coconut and canned tuna all got dumped in bowls of this dreadful chopped-up lettuce in vain attempts to make it look better. But it didn't fool very many, it was still undeniably lettuce, something to be stirred around with a fork and left on the side of the plate. It was always something that came with something, as in "that comes with fries or salad." There were Caesar salads, which used a different lettuce, the crunchy romaine, but most of us had learned early in life that salads were meant to be tasteless, and we weren't going to be fooled by somebody with a French accent stirring them around in a bowl with, of all things, *anchovies*.

Bill Jones is a chef who understands restaurant food. I've eaten his food in the world-famous Sooke Harbour House, at luxurious lodges, at fishing camps and in the country round a big alder fire slowly roasting a lamb. He's more than a chef, he's also a cook, of the "let's open the fridge and see what we've got" variety.

This book is written for cooks, for ordinary people who may have been seeing all manner of new and unfamiliar vegetables on the shelves of their markets but, still haunted by the ghosts of lettuce past, haven't had the courage to try them. As all good cookbooks should, it sets out a palate of flavors and textures that do good things for each other, and then leaves room for experimentation. I think he should have called it "Life after Lettuce."

James Barber
THE URBAN PEASANT

A Salad Primer

A Salad Primer

A salad can be a simple culinary act, like pulling a lettuce out of the ground, washing it, tossing it in a dressing and savoring the moment. With some effort and planning, a salad can be transformed into a speedy, healthy meal for the whole family. And with a dash of skill and determination, the humble salad can be elevated to a work of art, worthy to be served in the finest restaurants.

Fresh food is the best thing we can put in our bodies, and salad is the first thing that springs to mind when we think of fresh produce. Eating seasonally is the logical way to capitalize on our harvest of fresh food. In essence, we can get the maximum benefit from our food by eating seasonal, locally grown food.

Along with fresh produce, the other important part of salad is the flavoring (or dressings) we add. A traditional oil and vinegar dressing is sometimes all that is needed. Often a third element, mustard, is used to bring the flavors together in harmony. These three ingredients are actually wise choices: vinegar provides acidity, aiding digestion and providing many essential nutrients and vitamins; oil provides fat (energy and calories) and adds beneficial nutrients to the mix; and mustard is a powerful medicinal spice with many health-promoting effects. Served simply or with a wide array of seasonings — herbs, soy products, salt and pepper, to name a few — dressing adds a taste component that makes us want to eat our greens.

Salads are one way we can express our creativity and versatility. Endless variations are possible, merely by changing the combinations of greens, garnishes and dressings you toss in the salad bowl.

Local, Fresh Ingredients

Buy the best produce you can find. The oxygen we breathe is also the enemy of the nutrients in the food we eat. Oxidation speeds up the breakdown of food and creates products linked with many negative effects on our health. Nutrients start to deteriorate the moment the produce has been picked — so the freshness of food is critical to getting the maximum nutritional and health benefits from what we eat. It is worth the effort to seek out food that has just been harvested. Farm-gate sales, weekly markets, roadside stands and grocery stores that feature local produce are places to look for food, sometimes only hours away from the fields.

It is worth noting that local farmers also need our support. It's not easy to farm; it takes commitment, hard work and a lot of luck to successfully combat suburban encroachment, random acts of nature, health and legal issues.

The simple act of buying locally grown food has ripples that reach throughout the world. Every locally produced and consumed food is one less item whisked to us in trains and trucks, spewing exhaust fumes and heat. Sometimes it takes tiny steps to implement change on a global scale. Supporting local farmers can be a small, yet important, act and a catalyst for positive changes.

If local food is good, local organic food is the next step beyond. Food grown without the use of pesticides is easier on the environment, and it can affect a wide range of health issues. Yes, it might cost a little more than conventional food. Just ask yourself how much it is worth to make your life more vibrant and your health more robust.

Handle with Care

To make a great salad, you have to start with good ingredients. There is nowhere to hide inferior produce in a salad. When shopping for greens, look for leaves that are plump and blemish free. Heads should be tightly packed, with a hefty weight for their size. Avoid wilted greens, although you can try to bring them back to life by refreshing them in cold water. Prewashed and bagged greens, available in most grocery stores, can be great time-savers and are well worth trying (spinach packages seem particularly good). Occasionally they are treated with preservatives to increase the shelf life; read the labels carefully if you have allergies to these products.

Some lettuces are more robust than others; the delicate plants are often the first to wilt and decay when stored. Pick any wilted leaves out of a salad mix before use. Dense lettuce, like romaine and head varieties, will last many times longer than the delicate types.

When buying fresh greens, enjoy them the same day if possible. Soak greens in plenty of cold water to perk up the leaves. Simply place them in a bowl, cover with cold water and allow to sit for 5 minutes before draining. Pick out any badly wilted pieces. Remove excess moisture by drying in a salad spinner. Rolling the washed greens in paper towel (or a clean kitchen towel) also works well. Place the greens in the fridge to rest until needed. Chilling the greens for at least 20 minutes will yield perfect results.

For the maximum shelf life, wash and dry the leaves and place them in a container. Cover with a damp paper towel and seal with a lid. They will keep for 2 to 3 days in the fridge.

A Glossary of Greens

The following salad greens are listed in alphabetical order and reflect some of the most commonly used ingredients for salad mixes. Use the description to design a salad that has a balanced mix of flavor.

Arugula *(Eruca vesicaria)*
Spicy and strongly flavored; excellent with olive oil, garlic and tomatoes.

Arugula, rustic *(Eruca selvatica)*
Very spicy, similar to arugula with an added layer of flavor and spice.

Beet tops *(Beta vulgaris)*
Earthy and rich-tasting, great in a blend with blander ingredients like lettuce.

Belgian endive *(Cichorium intybus v. foliosum)*
Bitter, crisp and crunchy; excellent to balance a salad with rich components or dressing.

Bok choy *(Brassica rapa v. chinesis)*
Crisp, mild and juicy; excellent in Asian dishes. Dress just before serving as the dressing will tend to draw out the moisture in the flesh.

Cabbage, green *(Brassica oleracea v. capitata)*
Sweet and crisp when fresh; soft and crunchy when sautéed or marinated.

Chicory *(Cichorium intybus)*
Bitter and intense flavors; great with a sweet dressing of balsamic and olive oil.

Chard *(Beta vulgarius v. flavescens)*
Earthy and very similar to beet tops. Best when picked as young tender leaves.

Chickweed *(Stellaria media)*
Green, grassy and packed full of nutrition; excellent source of vitamins. Often found growing wild in gardens and in the cracks of sidewalks.

Claytonia *(Claytonia [or Montia] perfoliata)*
Green, slightly citrus flavors. A great addition to a salad bowl. Found wild throughout the Pacific Northwest or cultivated from seed.

Corn salad *(see Mache)*

Curly endive *(Cichorium endivia ssp. endivia)*
Slightly bitter, less so when blanched white. Also known as frisée, it is excellent for adding a bitter component to a salad mix. Wonderful when paired with rich smoked products like bacon, ham or salmon.

Dandelion *(Taraxacum officinale)*
Bitter edge, mild green flavor. Italian red variety is often grown as a salad and cooking herb. Best when young and mild; older specimens develop many bitter compounds.

Escarole *(Cichorium endivia)*
Bitter, hearty component to European salad mixes.

Frisée *(see Curly endive)*

Kale *(Brassica olenacea v. sabellica)*
Baby kale is sweet and tender; mature specimens are better suited for cooking. Very nutritious and particularly excellent in warm salads.

Lettuce *(Lactuca sativa)*
There are three main types of lettuce — head, romaine and leaf — and a mouth-watering array of varieties. The adventurous will find crunchy textures, frilly edges, sensual smoothness and intriguing bitter to spicy flavor highlights. Try the following varieties if you can find them.

- *Head*: Bibb, Iceberg, Ice Queen, Butterhead, Little Gem
- *Romaine*: Rouge d'Hiver, Brune d'Hiver, Freckles
- *Leaf*: Oakleaf, Red Oak, Lolla Rossa, Deer Tongue

Mache *(Valarianella locusta)*
Earthy, green flavors add interest and soft texture to a salad mix. Sometimes called corn salad.

Mibuna *(Brassica x. crucifera)*
Mildly spicy Japanese green; great in salad or as a cooked green.

Mint *(Mentha sp.)*
A little bit of mint adds an intriguing menthol edge to a salad mix, particularly those with bitter green components.

Minutina *(Plantago coronopus)*
Mildly bitter green also known as buckhorn plantain or erba stella. A traditional part of rustic Italian salads.

Mitsuba *(Petroselium sp.)*
Mildly aromatic Japanese green with a parsley-like flavor backed with a hint of celery. Use as a salad green or a cooked vegetable.

Mizuna *(Brassica rapa v. japonica)*
A mildly spicy Japanese green with a subtle mustard flavor. Use as a salad green or a cooked vegetable.

Mustard *(Brassica juncea)*
Spicy green or red leaves add zip to a salad; excellent in warm salads.

New Zealand spinach *(Tetragonia expansa)*
Green with a bitter edge and an attractive shape and color. Adds interest to any salad mix.

Orach *(Atriplex hortensis)*
Deep purple to red color and mild with a bitter edge. Partner with mild greens like lettuce for a fabulous contrast of taste and color.

Oxeye daisy leaves *(Leucanthemum vulgare)*
Green, floral, beautifully cut leaves. Flavor reminiscent of green apples and sage with a sweet aftertaste. Add young leaves to salad mixes or mixed into dressing and sauces.

Pea tops *(Pisum sativum)*
Sweet green flavor of fresh peas. The tender young plant tips are wonderful in a salad and extraordinary as a cooked vegetable (especially with lots of garlic!).

Perilla *(see Shiso)*

Purslane *(Portulaca oleracea)*
Rich flavor, high in minerals and Omega-3 fatty acids. Often found as a wild plant growing in rich, wet soils. One of the most nutritious plants in the garden.

Radicchio *(Cichorium intybus)*
Beautiful, mildly bitter, red and white leaves. Found in most commercial salad mixes for its rich color, long shelf life and balanced bitterness. Cooking (grilling or braising) removes a lot of the bitter components.

Shingiku *(Chrysanthemum coronarium)*
Floral, green flavor. This Japanese green is part of the chrysanthemum family and is a versatile salad and cooking green.

Shiso *(Perilla frutescens)*
Fragrant, spicy leaves. Red or green varieties have an exotic quality that is wonderful minced into a dressing. Great with seafood dishes and can be substituted in any dish calling for basil. Also known as perilla.

Spinach *(Spinacia oleracea* spp.*)*
Sweet green flavor, rich in vitamins, calcium and iron. Excellent on its own or mixed with other greens. The best all-round greens for warm salads.

Sui choy *(Brassica rapa v. parachinesis)*
Crisp, juicy, mild flavor. Also called napa cabbage. Add to salads just before serving as the dressing tends to draw out moisture. Cooks quickly and is a great addition to warm salads.

Tat soi *(Brassica rapa v. rosularis)*
Mild, spicy leaves form a beautiful rosette of round leaves. Excellent for salad mixes with a long shelf life. Great as a cooked vegetable.

Water cress *(Rorippa nasturtium-aquaticum)*
Peppery, juicy green leaves are strongly aromatic. Great on its own or mixed into a blend of milder greens.

Salad Mixes

Mixed greens
This is a catch-all phrase for traditional European salad mixes. They often contain different lettuce types along with bitter elements, like radicchio, and spicy elements, like arugula or mustard greens.

Mesclun
Mesclun is a traditional term for a mixture of wild and cultivated baby greens often including arugula, frisée, baby lettuces and salad herbs. Originating in the Provence region of France, mesclun was often used for the signature "Chef's Salad" in restaurants. In North America, mesclun was popularized by commercial growers in the southern USA. Here the usual mixes of traditional European greens (lettuce, kale and endive) were blended with Asian greens (like mizuna, tat soi and mustards). This fusion mix of the salad world is now widely sold in conventional grocery stores and is often available organically grown.

Custom salad greens
Small-scale commercial growers often blend a custom mix suited to local growing conditions and tastes. Mixes depend on availability and often change according to the season. Some mixes can contain up to 30 different greens and flowers. Choose clean, healthy-looking leaves. In addition to greens, you may find an array of herbs (fennel, marjoram, mint, basil, sorrel, etc.). The combinations are limitless.

Edible Flowers

Flowers add beauty and flavor to any salad mix. But be careful — many contain toxic compounds. Only eat those you can identify with certainty. In addition, flowers are often contaminated with toxins like pesticides and can absorb airborne pollutants (such as those near a busy roadway). Only eat organically grown flowers that you know are free of contamination.

Anise hyssop *(Agastache foeniculum)*
Pink flowers, licorice-flavored, fragrant and light.

Arugula *(Eruca vesicaria)*
Small, white, cross-shaped flowers with a spicy flavor.

Calendula *(Calendula officinalis)*
Orange, daisy-like petals with a slightly bitter flavor. Very beautiful in mixed salads, with a fairly long shelf life (petals dry quite easily). Also called pot marigold.

Chive *(Allium schoenoprasum)*
Large purple flower heads with small delicate petals and a mild onion flavor.

Dandelion *(Taraxacum officinale)*
Young flowers have a sweet, nectar-like flavor. As the flower ages it becomes increasingly bitter.

Day lily *(Hemerocallis* spp.)*
Sweet, vegetal flavor; an excellent addition to warm, Asian-flavored salads.

Dianthus *(Dianthus caryophyllus)*
Large showy pink flowers with a sweet, clove-like flavor. Also called pink carnation.

Johnny-jump-up *(Viola tricolor)*
Mild, small, mint-flavored flowers (some varieties taste like bubble gum!). Makes a pretty addition to any salad mix.

Nasturtium *(Tropaeolum* spp.*)*
Large flowers in a wide spectrum of colors, with a bright spicy flavor. Both flowers and leaves are used in many salad mixes.

Pansy *(Viola x wittrockiana)*
Petals are sweet and mild with green vegetal flavor. Pansies are available in a riot of colors from deep purple (almost black) to purple, red, pink and white (and many variegated forms). Wonderful as a last-minute addition to salad mixes.

Rose *(Rosa* spp.*)*
Perfumed floral petals (the scented varieties), used in moderation, make a bold statement in a salad mix.

Rosemary *(Rosmarinus officinalis)*
Large purple flower heads composed of many small blossoms; mild rosemary flavor.

Sage *(Salvia officinalis)*
Medium blossoms (similar to rosemary), usually pink or purple in color. Mild sage flavor.

Squash *(Cucurbita* spp.*)*
Large, orange, mildly vegetal flowers are usually sautéed or stuffed.

Tulip *(Tulipa* spp.*)*
Large multicolored petals, with an acidic (lemony) edge. Great as part of a salad mix or blended as part of the salad dressing.

Violet *(Viola odorata)*
Multicolored (deep violet to pink to white) petals with a delicate floral flavor. Good as a last-minute addition to salad mixes.

Vinegars

The word vinegar comes from the French *vin aigre* ("sour wine") and most good-quality culinary vinegar is the product of fermenting fruit juice of some kind. The main exception is rice wine vinegar, which is the product of fermenting rice. Common distilled white vinegar (from grain alcohol) is an industrial-age product, well suited for pickling and cleaning surfaces in your kitchen. For most recipes in this book, choose well-made wine, fruit or rice vinegar for the best results.

Most traditional vinegars are made through bacterial action. *Mycoderma aceti* forms what is known as a "mother" (or raft) on top of the fermenting liquid and converts the alcohol to acid. Most vinegars range from 4% to 7.5 % acidity. The higher the acidity, the stronger the effect of the vinegar on the flavor of the dressing.

The use of vinegar as a home medical remedy has been championed for years. It is said to aid in digestion (mixing well with our stomach acids) and is thought to play a beneficial role in keeping our joints healthy and moving freely.

Wine Vinegar

Balsamic vinegar

Native to the northern Italian region of Emilia-Romagna (and the city of Modena), balsamic vinegar is a precious culinary gift. At its best, good balsamic is like nectar. Made from the cooked juice of white Trebbiano grapes, balsamic vinegar gets its dark color from being aged (over several years) in a variety of wooden casks and finally blended with other vintages. The result is a sweet and sour elixir with big, mouth-watering flavor and a taste that can best be described as pure happiness. The price can be as incredible as the taste. A 1-oz. (28-mL) bottle of 25-year-old vinegar can cost hundreds of dollars. Bottles of 50-, 75- and even 100-year-old balsamic are available at atmospheric prices.

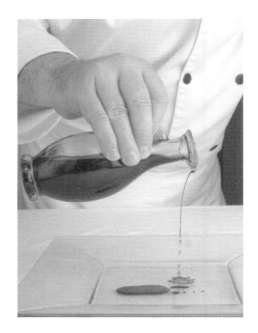

Commercially produced balsamic has an entirely different pedigree. Most of the balsamic sold in stores is fast-tracked through production and helped along with doses of fresh grape juice and caramel coloring. It still tastes good, but if you want the better qualities, look for the label *aceto balsamico tradizionale* (and be prepared to spend more money).

White balsamic is a modern marketing ploy and is essentially white wine vinegar sweetened with grape must. It has a good flavor and works well in most vinaigrettes, particularly when the aim is to preserve the vivid color of other ingredients.

White wine vinegar

Light and fruity, with a moderate acid level. It's great for all general-purpose dressings. Available in individual grape types like Chardonnay and Muscat.

Red wine vinegar

It's more robust than white wine vinegar, with a level of tannin that backs up the acidity. Great for salads with tomatoes and for stronger-flavored greens like chicory and mustard greens. Available in individual grape types like Pinot Noir and Zinfandel.

Champagne vinegar

A delicate, floral vinegar that adds refinement and elegance to salads. Wonderful when paired with delicate greens and any salad featuring seafood.

Sherry vinegar

Full-flavored, with overtones of caramel and dried fruit. Great when paired with salads that feature onion, potatoes or smoked products like ham or bacon.

Port vinegar

Rarely available, port vinegar is a real treat. Try with a salad using duck or game meats as an accent. A home-style version can be made by reducing 1 cup / 250 mL port by $1/4$ and adding it to 4 cups / 1 L of your favorite red wine vinegar.

Verjuice (or verjus)

Verjuice (or green juice) is naturally fermented vinegar made from the juice of unripe white, red or black grapes. Traditionally, Dijon mustards are made by blending verjuice, mustard paste, spices and salt. Muscat grapes make the most fragrant verjuice. Well-made verjuice starts life as moderately acidic, fruity, yeasty and sweet. In the crudest forms it can be relatively unstable and may become bitter and highly acidic; it should be used up fairly quickly after opening the bottle. It's great for marinating foods (meats, fish and poultry) and making mellow, fragrant dressing.

Fruit Vinegar

There are two main categories of fruit vinegars. Bulk, commercial vinegars are made by blending fruit extracts and flavorings with pure distilled vinegar. The best fruit vinegars are made from juice extracted from whole fruit. This second process is a laborious undertaking and some of the better fruit vinegars can be very expensive.

Apple cider vinegar

Apple is the most commonly available fruit vinegar. The best ones are made from unfiltered apple cider and are reputed to be beneficial tonics. Seek out cider vinegar made from organic apples for the best quality. Apple cider vinegar often has a bracing acidity that pairs well with honey in a dressing.

Raspberry vinegar

A staple of the French pantry, raspberry vinegar has a distinctive fruity and floral quality that pairs well with bitter greens.

Other fruit vinegars

If you are lucky you will find vinegars made from apricot, blackberry, blueberry, peach, pear and many other exotic fruits. All work well when a light, fruity, fragrant quality is desired.

Rice Vinegar

Cooked rice is fermented to produce alcohol (like sake) and the alcohol is then converted into vinegar. The best varieties are Japanese. Read the label carefully; many Japanese vinegars are preseasoned, such as sushi vinegar (with salt and sugar) or ponzu vinegar (with salt, mirin and citrus). They will make fine dressings but may throw off the balance of other ingredients in the dressing.

Beer Vinegar

In this age of micro and cottage breweries, a new class of artisan beer vinegars has emerged. Malty, hopping and full-flavored, choose these vinegars for potato salad and other robust dressings.

Infused Vinegar

Flavored vinegars are an expanding part of the modern marketplace. You can pay a hefty premium for a designer bottle and its contents — or you can easily make it at home. Use vinegar that has an acidity of over 5% (check the vinegar label). This gives an acidic environment that is inhospitable to the botulin spores (see "Infused oil," page 27). For quick infused vinegar, bring the vinegar to a boil in a nonreactive pan (stainless steel or ceramic coated) and add fruit, herbs, spices, chilies or mushrooms. Remove from the heat and allow to steep for 1 hour before straining and bottling.

The traditional, time-honored method is to crush the fruit and place it in a ceramic pot. Add vinegar (or "vinegar mold") and cover the crock with muslin (to keep out the fruit flies). The pot is kept in a cool dark place (like the cellar) and allowed to macerate for at least 6 months.

Oils

Not all oils are created equally. The type, chemical composition and age determines an oil's nutritional properties. The process of extraction is a second key element in the quality of oil. You usually get what you pay for, so buy the best quality of oil you can afford. In general, cold-pressed organic oils are the healthiest. They are made by mechanically pressing the ingredient to extract the oil. Cheaper oils are extracted by heating, grinding or chemical solvents and often have harsher flavors and fewer health benefits. Shelf life is an important consideration; oil oxidizes and breaks down into unhealthy components over time. Buy small amounts and consume the oil as soon as possible.

Oil composition is a huge topic and has far-reaching health implications. Oil is pure, liquid fat; each tablespoon (15 mL) has about 100 calories. It's also an essential element in our diets, responsible for fueling our bodies and contributing to the functions of our skin and organs. Depending on whether it is saturated, monounsaturated or polyunsaturated, oil can affect levels of good (HDL) cholesterol and bad (LDL) cholesterol. Oils also contain varying levels of Omega-3 fatty acids and vitamin E, both important to health. Another chemical component, poly-phenol, is touted as a powerful antioxidant and is attributed with many beneficial properties, from healing scarred arteries to lowering cholesterol, blood pressure and risk of coronary disease.

Heating has a huge impact on the properties of oil, often destroying healthy components and sometimes even altering the structure and creating unhealthy byproducts. Every oil has a specific smoke point — the temperature at which it will begin to smoke and give an unpleasant flavor to food. When using oil for deep frying, keep in mind that the smoke point is lowered each time the oil is heated (or even exposed to air). Use oils with the highest smoke points for cooking. Grapeseed oil is probably the best overall cooking oil; it has a light clean flavor and a very high smoke point (485°F / 252°C). Pure olive oil (460°F / 238°C) and canola (400°F / 200°C) are other good choices for cooking.

Storage of oil is another critical factor. Oil breaks down (oxidizes) over time into unhealthy trans fatty acids. This may be one of the most harmful aspects of processed foods containing oil. Store oil in a cool, dark place. Sunlight speeds up oxidation, so keep it in a dark place, out of the sunlight — or store in dark glass bottles. Oils with abundant organic material, like extra virgin olive oil (which contains chlorophyll) or infused oils, are particularly susceptible to oxidation. Homemade infused oil should be refrigerated and used within 2 to 3 days of preparation or frozen for up to 2 weeks. Polyunsaturated oils (particularly safflower) tend to oxidize more rapidly than other oils and are often stabilized with antioxidation agents. Under ideal conditions, most oil will easily last 1 year (from the production date) up to 3 years (depending on conditions and variety). If a stale, acrid aroma comes off the oil (and you can't remember when you put it in the cupboard!), chances are the oil has gone off. Oils high in polyunsaturates, such as safflower, should be refrigerated if you're keeping them more than a few months. Refrigeration will improve the shelf life of most oils. Olive oil will crystallize or solidify due to the presence of natural waxes, but warming the oil to room temperature will restore it to a liquid state.

Olive Oil

Olive oil is harvested and sold with much of the reverence reserved for wine. The two liquids are alike in that both occur in a wide range of quality and price. Olives are believed to have originated in the Middle East and eastern Mediterranean regions. The tree migrated into other areas of the world (most recently California and Australia) over time. Oils are graded primarily on the method of extraction and the presence of acids (mainly oleic acid). In general, mechanically extracted olive oils with low levels of acid are considered the finest. However, oils from northern areas, such as Tuscany, have naturally higher acid levels than oils produced in warmer climates and are still considered exceptionally fine. Freshly pressed oil from healthy olives has a very low acidity. Careless handling, disease and unripe fruit all contribute to raising the acidity which produces oil with harsh, bitter flavors. Olive oil is monounsaturated, has many health-promoting qualities and can be considered part of a healthy diet.

Experiment with different types of oil from a variety of regions, but remember to consume the older oils first, before they oxidize. Choosing oils can be a little confusing as there are differing standards and grading practices in various areas. Following are descriptions of the major categories accepted in North America and defined by the International Olive Oil Council.

Virgin olive oil

This is oil obtained only from olives (i.e. not blended with other oils) using mechanical and heat processes. It excludes oil obtained using chemical processes and is considered a natural product. Within this group there are many sub-categories based on taste, aroma and level of acidity.

- *Extra virgin olive oil* is a dark green oil that has a fragrant aroma and spicy aftertaste. Acidity levels must be 1% or less. This oil counts for less than 10% of total production in most countries and is consequently the most expensive oil available. It is often used to drizzle over finished salads (where a burst of intense olive flavor is appropriate) and makes a wonderful condiment for fresh bread — particularly with a little drizzle of balsamic vinegar.

- *Virgin olive oil* is similar to extra virgin but with a slightly higher acidity (maximum 2%) and a slight drop in the fruity, aromatic characteristics. It is great for making salad dressings and general cooking.

- *Ordinary virgin olive oil* has good flavor but lacks the flavor punch of the previous oils. Acidity (maximum 3.3%) is a little more pronounced and the flavor is subtler. Great for general cooking and dressings, particularly when the stronger oils might overpower a delicate food or seasoning.

Refined or blended olive oils

Outside the classification of virgin olive oils, there are many misleading and confusing labels that can trick consumers into buying an inferior grade of oil. These oils are acceptable for cooking and general purpose use.

- Pure olive oil is more correctly called refined olive oil. It is oil that has been refined (often with charcoal filtering or other chemical or physical filters) to eliminate defects such as high acidity or poor fruit quality. The maximum allowable acidity is .5%. Although this is similar to fine extra virgin oil, it has few of the aromatic characteristics and substantially less flavor. It is, however, a good cooking oil with a high smoke point.

- Oils simply labeled *olive oil* are actually a blend of refined and virgin oils. They have a maximum allowable acidity of 1.5% and are typically cheap refined olive oil that is blended with a flavorful virgin olive oil.

- *Pomace oil* is produced from the ground flesh and pits of the olive, after pressing to extract the best oils. Steam and solvents are usually used to extract the remaining oil. It is considered an inferior grade of oil and often chosen for cosmetic or industrial uses. It is sometimes mixed with refined olive oil and sold as olive pomace oil.

- *Monounsaturated fats* dominate the oils of many nuts, seeds and fruit like olives and avocado. The body can also readily burn the fat for energy. Oils high in these fats have been shown to have positive effects on, and in some degree improve, the health of our organs and tissue. Omega-3 and Omega-6 fatty acids are present in beneficial amounts and help promote a healthy cardiovascular system. Olive and canola oil are the most important members of this group. Current knowledge indicates we should make these the main oils in our diet.

- *Polyunsaturated fats* dominate in oils obtained from seeds like grape, sunflower, sesame, corn and soy. The body can convert some of these fats to saturated fats (to burn as fuel) and it uses other components to help protect organs and synthesize hormones. These oils are good for cooking (particularly those with high smoke points) as they are less prone to the unhealthy alterations that occur with the other fat types. Studies indicate polyunsaturated oils may contribute to lowering levels of unhealthy (LDL) cholesterol. These fats may also be prone to increased level of oxidation during long storage.

Light Oils

Grapeseed oil

This is one of the best all-round oils to use in the kitchen. Grapeseed oil is polyunsaturated and has less saturated fat than olive oil. It has a high burning point that makes it useful for cooking, contains significant levels of vitamin E and has a long shelf life. It has very little flavor and makes a neutral background for dressings or can be combined with more expensive oils (like nut oils) to extend (or dilute) the flavor. It is a great choice for making infused oils and salad dressing.

Canola oil

Canola is a valuable (although controversial) oil that is suitable for all types of cooking. Canola oil is pressed from a crop developed from the rapeseed plant. The oil of the original plant contained high levels of erucic acid, which has detrimental effects. Selective breeding produced a new generation of plant with a safe, low level of erucic acid. However, much of the canola now grown (particularly in Canada) has been genetically modified. Canola is a monounsaturated fat with very low levels of saturated fats (lower than olive oil). Moderate levels of polyunsaturated fats also help to make the profile of the oil very healthy. It is a good source of Omega-3 and Omega-6 fatty acids and may help lower unhealthy blood cholesterol levels (particularly when it replaces saturated fat in the diet). Canola is an excellent neutral-flavored base for blending or infusing and has a high smoke point.

Other light oils

Safflower, sunflower and corn oil are all acceptable as salad ingredients. These are polyunsaturated oils and prone to oxidation over time. Buy smaller bottles of these oils, store them in a dark cool place away from sources of heat and use them up quickly.

Toasted Oils

Sesame oil

Toasted sesame oil complements most Asian-inspired flavors. The best oils generally come from Japan and have a golden brown color and a light fragrant nose. Chinese sesame oils are sometimes very dark (over-roasted or from inferior seed) with a harsh edge to the aroma (some can be positively vile, so be careful). No matter what kind you use, too much sesame oil can overpower a dish. Start with a few drops and adjust to taste. Untoasted sesame oil is also available and has a mild, neutral flavor. Look for cold-pressed oils for the maximum health benefits. Sesame oil has an excellent shelf life.

Pumpkin seed oil

The seeds are gently toasted and cold pressed to yield deep green oil that is rich in vitamins, minerals and proteins. The flavor is nutty and smoky. Slightly reminiscent of extra virgin olive oil, it can be used interchangeably in recipes calling for a drizzle of olive oil and balsamic vinegar. Too much pumpkin seed oil can be overpowering, so use it with caution, or dilute with an equal volume of light oil (such as grapeseed or canola). The oil has a low burning point and is unsuitable for frying. Pumpkin seed oil also readily stains fabric, so be careful with those white linens! Occasionally, untoasted pumpkin oil is available.

Nut Oils

Almond, hazelnut, peanut (actually a tuber) and pecan are excellent monounsaturated oils. Walnut oil is polyunsaturated. The flavor of each nut type comes through in the oils, which adds a wonderful richness to salad dressings. Nut oils generally have a high smoke point and can be used in cooking. They are usually expensive; if desired you can blend with a little grapeseed oil to extend the flavor (although it will also diminish it). Be sure to tell guests if you use nut oil, as nut allergies are severe and fairly common. The oil goes rancid quickly if exposed to heat and sunlight; store it in the fridge.

Infused Oils

Infused oils have flooded the markets in recent years. Some are excellent; others are weak and can even be repugnant. Oil has a limited shelf life and adding organic material sometimes speeds up the process of decay. Often the date of manufacture is not stamped on the label and you may be buying a beautiful and expensive bottle of rancid oil. The best approach is to buy from a retailer you know and trust (and one who has a high rate of turnover on stock).

Infused oil can also be a perfect medium to grow harmful bacteria like botulism spores. Manufacturers usually increase the acidity of the oil to prevent bacterial growth. For safety, all infused oils should be refrigerated. Consume commercial infused oils within 2–3 weeks.

It is a simple matter to make your own infused oils at home. The quickest method is to process the ingredients using a blender, food processor or immersion blender. To begin, sterilize all equipment (run it through the dishwasher) before use. Keep your hands very clean (it helps to wear latex gloves) and rinse with vinegar or lemon juice before starting. Add any of the following to 1 cup (250 mL) of oil and process as described below.

- ¼ cup (60 mL) chopped fresh herbs (use one or combine basil, chives, rosemary, sage, thyme, etc.)

- 1 Tbsp. (15 mL) hot chilies (fresh or dried)

- 2 Tbsp. (30 mL) spices, toasted and ground (curry powder, star anise, fennel, cinnamon, pepper, etc.)

- 1 cup (250 ml) crustacean shells (crab, lobster, shrimp)

- 2 Tbsp. (30 mL) ground, dried wild mushrooms (porcini, pine mushrooms, truffles, etc.)

For the fresh herbs and chilies: Purée the oil and ingredients. Allow to steep for 1 hour. Strain the oil through a fine sieve or cheese-cloth and transfer into a glass jar. Seal and refrigerate until needed. Use within 2–3 days. Oil can be frozen in small containers for 1–2 weeks. The purée left from straining can be used in cooking.

For the spices, shells and mushrooms: Place the oil and seasoning in a saucepan over low heat for 15–20 minutes. Remove from the heat and allow to cool. Strain the oil through a fine sieve or cheese-cloth and transfer into a glass jar. Seal and refrigerate until needed. Use within 2–3 days. Oil can be frozen in small containers for 1–2 weeks.

Mustards

Mustard is the key to a lot of great salad dressing. The purée enhances the emulsion of oil and vinegar — helping to coat the greens and stimulating the taste buds. Mustard has a long history as a medicinal spice. It is thought to help promote circulation, and a good sniff of strong mustard can help clear clogged sinuses.

Most prepared mustard is made with two types of seeds. White mustard seed is the mellower of the two and is used for most commercially prepared mustard pastes. It is favored for its chemical stability and tends to separate less when prepared as a paste. Brown (sometimes called "black") mustard seeds are more pungent and hot and are used to make English mustard powder and fine regional French and German mustards. It should be noted that pure mustard oil contains high levels of erucic acid and is banned for consumption in many parts of the world. It must be heated at high temperature to negate the effects of the acid and should never be used for salad dressings.

Many of the recipes in this book call for a pungent base of mustard. You can easily adjust the amount to fit your personal taste. You can also vary the type of mustard to complement or contrast with the other salad ingredients. For example, if a salad mix contains a lot of bitter greens, balance the dressing by using sweet mustard (like those made with honey).

American-style prepared mustard
Made from white mustard seeds and tinted bright yellow with the addition of turmeric. Good for many dressings, with a mild, acidic flavor and vibrant color.

Dijon mustard
Hulled black mustard, originally from the Dijon region of France. Puréed seeds are cooked with white wine (or verjuice), seasonings and salt. The flavor is a little salty and can be hotter than American-style prepared mustard. Marries well with herb-based dressings.

German mustard
There are two main types: Düsseldorf-style brown seed mustard (similar to Dijon) locally called Löwensenf (lion's mustard), and a sweet Bavarian-style mustard made from coarsely ground white mustard seeds, honey and herbs.

Grainy mustard
Usually Dijon-style mustard made with a combination of hulled and unhulled brown mustard seeds. A wonderful texture and burst of true mustard flavor.

Honey mustard
Dijon or American-style mustard sweetened with honey. A beautiful foil for strong-flavored vinegars (particularly apple cider). Be sure to monitor dressings calling for a sweetener if you are using honey mustard — you may need to add a dash more vinegar or citrus to compensate.

Horseradish mustard
Dijon, Russian or American-style mustards with horseradish added for heat. The spiciness varies dramatically with different brands. Particularly good with recipes calling for beets.

English mustard
Powdered mustard made from ground brown mustard seeds, mustard flour and wheat flour (added to improve texture). The most famous brand is Colman's. In dressing recipes, start with half the amount specified (for paste mustard), and adjust to taste.

Russian mustard
Russian (or Eastern European) mustard is an intriguing hot brown mustard paste usually with a sweet, balanced finish from added sugar or honey. It is wonderful with Asian flavors and works well with cabbage and tomato-based salads.

Vinaigrettes and Creamy Dressings

The Good Dressing Guide

Making a salad dressing is like playing a musical instrument. Once you've got the basic notes you open up a whole world of beautiful improvisation. Store-bought dressings are fine in a pinch but they are often full of preservatives and stabilizers. Homemade dressings are a quick and healthy way to spice up your salads. Salad dressings can be divided into two general types — vinaigrettes and creamy dressings.

The basic vinaigrette is a tart marriage of oil and vinegar (or acidic liquid), seasoned with a wide assortment of flavorings (often including mustard). The method is simple: put all the flavoring ingredients into a bowl and mix to an even consistency, slowly whisk in the oil to make an emulsion, and season with salt and pepper. You may want to thin the dressing with a little additional liquid (water is always fine).

Creamy dressings are made from a base of dairy, soy, mayon-naise, nuts or seeds. Dairy makes the creamiest dressings, usually in the form of sour cream or yogurt, followed by mayonnaise (an emulsion of egg yolk, vinegar and oil), then nuts, seeds and soy products. The richness of the dressing is used to balance the recipe (as a foil to an acidic ingredient like tomatoes), to complement a soft and sensual texture like spinach or to enrich a bland starch like potato.

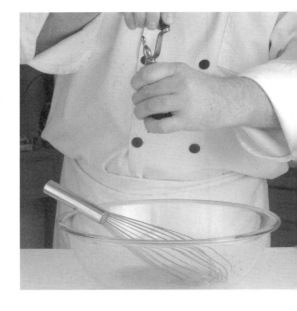

Italian Greens with a Roasted Pepper Dressing   p. 58

Baby Lettuce with Blackberry-Ginger Vinaigrette   p. 47

Spinach Salad with Japanese Seasonings   p. 52

Lettuce Wedges with Creamy Hazelnut Pesto   p. 50

You can also use a jar or plastic container to shake the dressing into a smooth consistency — just make sure that the lid is on tight! The container should be no more than $^2/_3$ full. For large quantities of dressing, it's always better to use a blender or submersible blending wand. These power tools make the job quick and easy, rapidly incorporate the flavors and create a strong emulsion. If you are using herbs and want to retain the texture, hand chop them and add them after blending. Add spicy flavors after blending to avoid overspicing (particularly the first time you make the recipe). Adding garlic after blending will result in a mellower flavor.

Most dressing recipes in this book yield about $^1/_2$ cup (125 mL). Use only enough dressing to lightly coat the salad. Serve the rest on the side for those who want more, or reserve for another use. A good restaurant tip is to drizzle a little extra dressing around the salad for a colorful presentation. Fresh dressing can be made up in bulk by doubling or quadrupling the recipes. Just before the final seasoning of salt and pepper, adjust the consistency of the dressing with a little liquid, such as water, to obtain a nice pouring consistency. Refrigerate in a sealable jar for up to 1 week for vinaigrettes and 2–3 days for dairy-based dressings.

Basic Vinaigrette

2 Tbsp. / 30 mL **wine vinegar**

2 Tbsp. / 30 mL **water**

¼ cup / 60 mL **extra virgin olive oil**

salt and black pepper to taste

Place the vinegar and water in a small mixing bowl. Drizzle in the oil, whisking constantly, until smooth and thick.

Season with salt and pepper and set aside until needed.

VARIATIONS

Substitute any oil (such as nut oils) or vinegar (such as balsamic) of your choice, or use juice, cider or wine in place of the water. You can also boost the flavor by adding a minced clove of garlic.

PLAYING WITH ACIDITY

The percentage of acid in the vinegar will affect the overall sharpness of an oil and vinegar dressing. Balsamic vinegar is sweet and sour, rice vinegar is mild, wine vinegar is medium and apple cider vinegar is fairly strong. You can also vary the ratio of vinegar to oil: 25% vinegar to oil will be mellow, 50% vinegar will be medium and 75% vinegar to oil will be sharp. If the dressing tastes flat, add more vinegar. If it tastes too acidic, whisk in a little more oil.

Mustard Vinaigrette

1 Tbsp. / 15 mL Dijon mustard
1 Tbsp. / 15 mL wine vinegar
2 Tbsp. / 30 mL water
¹/₄ cup / 60 mL extra virgin olive oil
salt and black pepper to taste

Place the mustard, vinegar and water in a small mixing bowl. Drizzle in the oil, whisking constantly, until smooth and thick.

Season with salt and pepper and set aside until needed.

VARIATIONS

Vary the type of mustard, vinegar, oil or liquid, or boost the flavor by adding a minced clove of garlic.

EMULSIONS

An emulsion occurs when oil and vinegar (two liquids of different densities) are mixed together and the liquid breaks up into microscopic droplets of oil suspended in the vinegar. Over time the droplets will separate and the oil will float to the top. Just before serving, simply whisk or shake it again to form a smooth emulsion. Mustard, mayonnaise, purées and dairy products such as sour cream will stabilize the emulsion. A blender will break the oil into the smallest particles and make a long-lasting emulsion.

Herb Vinaigrette

1 Tbsp. / 15 mL mustard

1 Tbsp. / 15 mL vinegar

1 Tbsp. / 15 mL minced fresh herbs

1 Tbsp. / 15 mL water

¼ cup / 60 mL light oil

salt and black pepper to taste

Place the mustard, vinegar, herbs and water in a mixing bowl. Whisking constantly, drizzle in the oil until the mixture is smooth and thick.

Season with salt and pepper and set aside until needed.

VARIATIONS

Basic herbs: basil, chives, cilantro, marjoram, mint, rosemary, sage, tarragon, thyme.

Exotic herbs: arugula, chocolate mint, fruit sage, lemon balm, lemon thyme, pineapple sage, purple basil, shiso.

HERBAL MAGIC

Fresh herbs are a fantastic way to boost the flavor of salad dressing. Regular varieties of basil, marjoram, rosemary, sage and thyme are available in many markets. Try to think of the aromatic qualities of the herb (fragrant, spicy, sweet, lemony) and attempt to match it with the other ingredients in the salad. Be careful with overpowering herbs like lemon balm, lavender and tarragon. I try not to use dried herbs in a salad dressing; if fresh herbs are not available, try a little minced green onion instead.

Balsamic-Honey Vinaigrette

MAKES ½ CUP (125 mL)

2 Tbsp. / 30 mL **balsamic vinegar**

1 Tbsp. / 15 mL **honey**

1 tsp. / 5 mL **minced garlic**

1 Tbsp. / 15 mL **water**

¼ cup / 60 mL **olive oil**

salt and black pepper to taste

Place the vinegar, honey, garlic and water in a small mixing bowl. Drizzle in the oil, whisking constantly, until smooth and thick.

Season with salt and pepper and set aside until needed.

VARIATIONS

Substitute maple syrup or brown sugar for the honey; use chilies, herbs or citrus zest instead of the garlic.

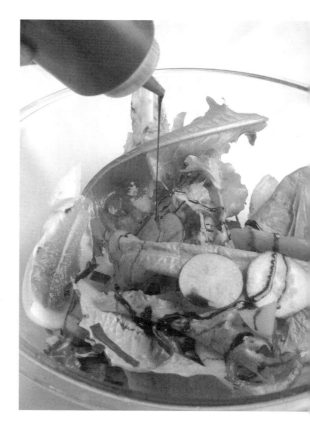

Lemon-Ginger Vinaigrette

MAKES ½ CUP (125 ML)

1 lemon, juice and zest

1 Tbsp. / 15 mL minced ginger

¼ cup / 125 mL light oil

salt and black pepper to taste

Place the lemon juice, zest and ginger in a mixing bowl. Drizzle in the oil, whisking constantly, until smooth and thick.

Season with salt and pepper and set aside until needed.

VARIATIONS

Substitute grapefruit, lime, orange or other citrus for the lemon.

ZESTING

The outer peel, or zest, of citrus fruit contains many volatile oils that can add a potent punch to dressings. Peel off strips of this flavorful skin, leaving behind the bitter white pith underneath. A tool called a citrus zester is designed to peel the outer layer in long strands. More recently, finely meshed stainless steel graters have become available. They also do a great job on ginger and garlic and are a useful tool for the pantry.

Berry Vinaigrette

¹/₄ cup / 60 mL **berry purée** (blackberry,
  blueberry, raspberry, etc.)
2 Tbsp. / 30 mL **white wine vinegar** (or lemon juice)
2 Tbsp. / 30 mL **light oil**
salt and black pepper to taste

Place the berry purée and vinegar in a mixing bowl. Drizzle in the
oil, whisking constantly, until smooth and thick.

Season with salt and pepper and set aside until needed.

VARIATION

Use any fruit purée (such as apple, pear, peach, plum). Purées of sweet vegetables (such as carrot, pea, beet) also work well.

PURÉES

Berry purées can easily be made by puréeing fresh or frozen fruit in a food processor (or blender). Thin with just enough water to make the mixture smooth. Strain through a fine mesh sieve to obtain a purée free of seeds. Thin dense purées with a little additional water to make straining a little easier. If using frozen berries, add a little fresh lemon juice to the purée to mask the flavor caused by tannins in the skin. For convenience, make a batch of purée and freeze. Freezing the purée in an ice cube tray gives blocks of about 2 Tbsp. (30 mL). After freezing, transfer the cubes to a resealable bag. Simply defrost the amount you need for the recipe. Excellent purées can be purchased ready to use (often sold in tetra-packs or as frozen blocks). Tart purées like red and black currants, gooseberries and cranberries may need a little extra sweetener to balance the acidity. In a pinch, a spoonful of your favorite jam makes a good substitute for berry purées. Just be sure to taste and adjust the sweetness with a dash more vinegar.

Soy-Mustard Vinaigrette

1 Tbsp. / 15 mL mustard

1 Tbsp. / 15 mL rice vinegar

2 Tbsp. / 30 mL light soy sauce

1 Tbsp. / 15 mL honey

¼ cup / 60 mL light oil

salt and black pepper to taste

Place the mustard, vinegar, soy sauce and honey in a mixing bowl. Drizzle in the oil, whisking constantly, until smooth and thick.

Season with salt and pepper and set aside until needed.

VARIATIONS

Substitute reduced-sodium soy, dark soy, tamari soy, sweet soy, miso paste, hoisin sauce or black bean paste for the light soy sauce.

SOYBEAN SAUCES AND PASTES

Many wonderful Asian condiments are now widely available. Look in the ethnic food aisle of your favorite grocery store or seek out Asian specialty markets. Many sauces and seasonings are made from the soybean, one of the most nutrient-rich foods available.

Soy sauce was probably devised as a way of preserving food. The sauce is generally made by fermenting ground soybeans, roasted wheat (or other grains), salt and yeast. The main types are light and dark soy. The light is often saltier (unless it is labeled as reduced-sodium) and is used for flavoring most foods. Dark soy has added molasses, is often less salty and is used extensively for cooking. Sweet soy (or kecap manis) is a flavored Indonesian-style soy sauce that is fermented with sugar syrup.

Black bean paste is made from fermented and salted black soybeans. It is a common seasoning in Chinese cuisines. For convenience, use the prepared black bean sauces available. Check the label; many brands have MSG added and some are very salty.

Hoisin sauce is a sweet rich purée made from a paste of soy beans, sometimes mixed with yam, and spices (often the famous five-spice mixture). Miso is a fermented soybean paste (see page 63).

Caesar Dressing

1 Tbsp. / 15 mL minced garlic

1 tsp. / 5 mL minced anchovy or anchovy paste

1 Tbsp. / 15 mL Worcestershire sauce

2 Tbsp / 30 mL mayonnaise

1 tsp. / 5 mL hot sauce

1 lemon, juice and zest

1 Tbsp. / 15 mL water

¼ cup / 60 mL extra virgin olive oil

1 Tbsp. / 15 mL grated Parmesan cheese

salt and black pepper to taste

Place the garlic, anchovy, Worcestershire sauce, mayonnaise, hot sauce, lemon juice, zest and water in a mixing bowl. Drizzle in the oil, whisking constantly, until smooth and thick. Add the cheese and whisk to blend.

Note: If you use a blender to make this recipe, add the cheese after puréeing to retain more texture.

Season with salt and pepper and set aside until needed.

VARIATIONS

Substitute minced olives or herbs for the anchovy; use balsamic vinegar, wine vinegar, sherry vinegar or apple cider vinegar for the lemon.

PARMESAN CHEESE

Parmesan has come to be a generic term for cow's milk cheese mass-produced in many parts of the world. True Parmesan cheese is a hard, dry cow's milk cheese with a nutty, rich flavor made in the Emilia-Romagna region of Italy. The name Parmigiano-Reggiano is branded on the rind and its use is tightly controlled. Other hard cheeses of the region are defined as Grana (the most famous is Grana Padano — from the Po valley). It is still made in small batches, according to methods that have been followed for 800 years. The longer the cheese is aged, the more granular and flavorful it becomes. Aged Parmesan is relatively low in cholesterol and saturated fats. It is nutty and fragrant, and its flavor is light-years away from the mass-produced variety.

Apple Cider Dressing

1 Tbsp. / 15 mL **apple cider vinegar**

1 tsp. / 5 mL **minced garlic**

2 Tbsp. / 30 mL **mayonnaise**

1 tsp. / 5 mL **hot sauce**

1 Tbsp. / 15 mL **apple juice (or water)**

¼ cup / 60 mL **vegetable oil**

salt and black pepper to taste

Place the vinegar, garlic, mayonnaise, hot sauce and juice in a mixing bowl. Drizzle in the oil, whisking constantly, until smooth and thick.

Season with salt and pepper and set aside until needed.

Spinach and Sour Cream Dressing

MAKES ABOUT ½ CUP (125 mL)

1 lemon, juice and zest

¼ cup / 60 mL sour cream

1 tsp. / 5 mL minced garlic

1 tsp. / 5 mL hot sauce

¼ cup / 60 mL blanched spinach (or frozen, thawed and drained)

salt and black pepper to taste

Place the lemon juice, zest, sour cream, garlic and hot sauce in a blender. Process the mixture until smooth.

Squeeze any excess water from the spinach and drop it into the blender. Pulse to a smooth green purée. Thin with a little water, if necessary, to make a pouring consistency. Season with salt and pepper and set aside until needed.

VARIATIONS

Substitute coconut milk for the sour cream and add 1 tsp. (5 mL) curry paste.

BLANCHING SPINACH

Spinach is a great way to add a pure green color to any dressing, sauce or soup. Blanching (partially cooking) the greens in boiling, salted water helps to set a vivid green color and makes it easy to purée. Add about 1 tsp. (5 mL) salt for each 4 cups (1 L) of water. Cook until soft and still a vivid green, about 2–3 minutes. Remove from the water and cool quickly in a bowl of water and ice. Drain well and squeeze in the hand to remove as much moisture as possible.

Green Salads

Shredded Lettuce with Sesame-Balsamic Dressing

2 Tbsp. / 30 mL **balsamic vinegar**

1 Tbsp. / 15 mL **soy sauce**

1 tsp. / 5 mL **sesame oil**

1 Tbsp. / 15 mL **water**

$^1/_4$ cup / 60 mL **light oil**

salt and black pepper to taste

. . . .

1 large head **iceberg (or romaine) lettuce**

1 Tbsp. / 15 mL **toasted sesame seeds**

Place the vinegar, soy sauce, sesame oil and water in a mixing bowl. Drizzle in the light oil, whisking constantly, until the mixture is smooth and thick. Season with salt and pepper and set aside until needed.

Rinse the lettuce; separate it into individual leaves and dry. Chill until needed.

On a cutting board, roll the lettuce into a loose bundle and slice thinly into strips. Place the greens in a salad bowl, coat lightly with the dressing and toss well. Sprinkle the sesame seeds on top and serve immediately.

TOASTING SEEDS AND NUTS

Seeds and nuts have volatile elements that may become stale as they are stored. Toasting removes excess moisture, revives the flavor and restores crispness. Place the seeds or nuts in a dry skillet over medium-high heat. Shake the pan to toss the contents and evenly distribute the heat. If the seeds or nuts begin to scorch, reduce the heat and quickly toss to cool. Cook until evenly golden brown and immediately transfer to a plate to cool. Toasting in the oven on a baking sheet is another option but it is easy to forget and often results in burnt seeds or nuts.

Baby Lettuce with Blackberry-Ginger Vinaigrette

SERVES 4

2 Tbsp. / 30 mL **balsamic vinegar**

2 Tbsp. / 30 mL **blackberry purée**

1 tsp. / 5 mL **grated ginger**

1 Tbsp. / 15 mL **water**

2 Tbsp. / 30 mL **light oil**

salt and black pepper to taste

. . . .

1 lb. / 450 g **mixed baby lettuce (or salad mix)**

Place the vinegar, blackberry purée, ginger and water in a mixing bowl. Drizzle in the oil, whisking constantly, until the mixture is smooth and thick. Season with salt and pepper and set aside until needed.

Rinse the greens; rip larger pieces into bite-size chunks and dry. Chill until needed.

Place the greens in a mixing bowl, coat lightly with the dressing and toss well. Serve immediately.

Caesar Salad with Parmesan Croutons

1 large **head romaine (or iceberg) lettuce**

1 recipe **Caesar Dressing (page 41)**

1 Tbsp. / 15 mL **shredded Parmesan cheese**

1 Tbsp. / 15 mL **shredded anchovies (optional)**

1 recipe **Parmesan Croutons**

freshly ground black pepper

Rinse the romaine; rip it into bite-size chunks and dry. Chill until needed.

Place the lettuce in the salad bowl, coat lightly with the dressing and toss well. Garnish with the grated cheese and chopped anchovies (if desired). Top with croutons, add a sprinkling of pepper and serve immediately.

VARIATIONS

Substitute chopped olives, roasted bell pepper or roasted garlic for the anchovies.

Parmesan Croutons

MAKES 1 CUP (250 ML)

1 cup / 250 mL **cubed stale bread**

2 Tbsp. / 30 mL **olive oil**

1 tsp. / 5 mL **minced garlic**

2 Tbsp. / 30 mL **grated Parmesan cheese**

salt and black pepper to taste

Place the bread in a frying pan over medium-high heat and drizzle with the olive oil. When the pan is sizzling and the croutons are beginning to brown, add the garlic and toss well to mix. After 1 minute, add the cheese and toss to coat. Remove from the heat and season with salt and pepper. Place the croutons on a plate covered with paper towel to absorb any excess oil. Cool the croutons to room temperature.

Romaine Salad with Toasted Sunflower Dressing

$^1/_2$ cup / 125 mL **toasted sunflower seeds**

1 tsp. / 5 mL **minced garlic**

1 tsp. / 5 mL **hot sauce**

1 tsp. / 5 mL **honey**

1 Tbsp. / 15 mL **rice vinegar (or white wine vinegar)**

2 Tbsp. / 30 mL **water**

salt and black pepper to taste

. . . .

1 large head **romaine (or iceberg) lettuce**

2 Tbsp. / 30 mL **toasted sunflower seeds**

1 Tbsp. / 30 mL **minced fresh parsley**

Place the sunflower seeds, garlic, hot sauce, honey, vinegar and water in a blender. Process the mixture until smooth and season with salt and pepper. Thin with a little water, if necessary, to make a pouring consistency. Set aside until needed.

Rinse the lettuce; rip into bite-size chunks and dry. Chill until needed.

Place the lettuce in the salad bowl and coat lightly with the dressing. Toss well. Garnish with the sunflower seeds and parsley and serve immediately.

Lettuce Wedges with Creamy Hazelnut Pesto

$^1/_4$ cup / 60 mL chopped toasted hazelnuts

1 Tbsp. / 15 mL minced garlic

1 Tbsp. / 15 mL balsamic vinegar

2 Tbsp. / 30 mL mayonnaise

2 Tbsp. / 30 mL water

$^1/_4$ cup / 60 mL light oil

salt and black pepper to taste

. . . .

1 large head iceberg or romaine lettuce

2 Tbsp. / 30 mL chopped, toasted hazelnuts

Place the hazelnuts, garlic, vinegar, mayonnaise, water and oil in a blender. Process until it's well blended but still has a little texture from the nuts. Thin with a little water, if necessary, to make a pouring consistency. Chill until needed.

Remove the core from the lettuce, cut it in half and rinse under cold running water. Shake it dry, roll it in paper towel and chill until needed.

Place the lettuce on a cutting board and cut each half into 4 wedges. Place a wedge on each plate and place a second wedge over the middle of the first. Drizzle with dressing, garnish with chopped hazelnuts and serve immediately.

VARIATIONS

Substitute any other nut for the hazelnuts or use commercial nut butter (available in most grocery stores). Use 2 Tbsp. (30 mL) nut butter in place of the chopped nuts in the dressing.

Lettuce with Green Goddess Dressing

SERVES 4

1 lemon, juice and zest

1 Tbsp. / 15 mL chopped fresh tarragon

2 Tbsp. / 30 mL chopped fresh chives

2 Tbsp. / 30 mL chopped fresh parsley

1 tsp. / 5 mL minced garlic

2 Tbsp. / 30 mL sour cream

2 Tbsp. / 30 mL water

1 Tbsp. / 15 mL olive oil

salt and black pepper to taste

. . . .

1 large head lettuce (such as Lolla Rossa or Bibb)

1 recipe Garlic Croutons

1 Tbsp. /15 mL chopped fresh chives

Place the lemon juice, zest, tarragon, 2 Tbsp. /30 mL chives, parsley, garlic, sour cream, water and oil in a blender. Process until well blended. Thin with a little water, if necessary, to make a pouring consistency. Season well with salt and pepper and chill until needed.

Rinse the lettuce; rip into bite-size chunks and dry. Chill until needed.

Place the lettuce in a salad bowl, lightly coat with dressing and toss well. Garnish with the croutons and the 1 Tbsp /15 mL chives and serve immediately.

Garlic Croutons

MAKES 1 CUP (250 ML)

1 cup / 250 mL cubed stale bread

2 Tbsp. / 30 mL olive oil

1 Tbsp. / 15 mL minced garlic

salt and black pepper to taste

Place the bread in a frying pan over medium-high heat and drizzle with the olive oil. When the pan is sizzling and the croutons are beginning to brown, add the garlic and toss well to mix. Cook for an additional minute, remove from the heat and season with salt and pepper. Place the croutons on a plate covered with paper towel to absorb the excess oil. Cool the croutons to room temperature.

Spinach Salad with Japanese Seasonings

2 Tbsp. / 30 mL shredded pickled ginger

1 Tbsp. / 15 mL rice vinegar

2 Tbsp. / 30 mL mayonnaise

2 Tbsp. / 30 mL water

1 tsp. / 5 mL sesame oil

1 Tbsp. / 15 mL light soy sauce

1 tsp. / 5 mL wasabi paste (or to taste)

salt and black pepper to taste

. . . .

1 lb. / 450 g spinach, washed and dried

1 bunch mustard sprouts (or bean, sunflower or daikon sprouts)

1 sheet nori, cut in long, thin strips

1 Tbsp. / 15 mL furitake seasoning (or toasted sesame seeds)

Place the pickled ginger, vinegar, mayonnaise, water, sesame oil, soy sauce and wasabi paste in a mixing bowl and stir until well combined. Season lightly with salt and pepper and chill until needed.

Place the spinach in a salad bowl, lightly coat with dressing and toss well. Garnish with the sprouts, nori and furitake and serve immediately.

NORI AND FURITAKE SEASONINGS
Seaweed is a very nutritious vegetable and worthy of a larger role in our diets. Nori sheets are commonly used in sushi dishes to wrap bundles of rice and fish or to season other Japanese dishes. The best varieties are deep emerald green. Nori is commonly known in the West as *laver*. Furitake is a prepared Japanese seasoning mixture of nori flakes and sesame seeds with a variety of other delicacies. Dashi (dried bonito tuna) flakes and dehydrated wasabi (Japanese horseradish) are popular additives. Many varieties contain MSG. Read the label and be prepared to pay more for the additive-free varieties.

Butter Lettuce with Blue Cheese Dressing

SERVES 4

1 Tbsp. / 15 mL chopped garlic

2 Tbsp. / 30 mL mayonnaise

1 lemon, juice only

2 Tbsp. / 30 mL water

$1/4$ cup / 60 mL crumbled blue cheese

1 Tbsp. / 15 mL chopped fresh parsley

salt and black pepper to taste

. . . .

4 small heads butter lettuce

1 recipe Garlic Croutons (page 51)

additional crumbled blue cheese for garnish

2 Tbsp / 30 mL chopped toasted nuts, such as pecans,
   walnuts, etc. (optional)

Place the garlic, mayonnaise, lemon juice, water, cheese and parsley in a blender. Process until well blended. Thin with a little water, if necessary, to make a pouring consistency. Season well with salt and pepper and chill until needed.

Rinse the lettuce; rip it into bite-size chunks and dry. Chill until needed.

Place one whole lettuce on each plate and drizzle with the dressing. Garnish with the croutons and a sprinkling of crumbled cheese and chopped nuts (if desired). Serve immediately.

THE CHEESE BLUES

Originally cheeses were stored in natural caves, with near-perfect conditions of constant temperature and humidity. The caves also provided fertile grounds for a multitude of natural yeasts and molds. One of these molds, *Penicillium roqueforti*, is responsible for most of our wonderful blue cheeses. Modern cheesemakers help along the process and mix the mold into milk as it is processed. Roquefort, Stilton and Gorgonzola are the most famous varieties, but a number of fantastic blue cheeses are available. More recently, local artisan cheesemakers are turning out increasingly sophisticated blue cheeses. Check out your local market for examples of good, regional blue cheese.

Frisée with Grainy Mustard and Maple Dressing

2 Tbsp. / 30 mL balsamic vinegar

1 Tbsp. / 15 mL maple syrup

1 Tbsp. / 15 mL grainy mustard

1 Tbsp. / 15 mL water

$^{1}/_{4}$ cup / 60 mL light oil

salt and black pepper to taste

. . . .

4 cups / 1 L frisée (or endive, salad mix, etc.)

1 recipe Garlic Bread Crumbs (page 60)

Place the vinegar, maple syrup, mustard and water in a mixing bowl. Drizzle in the oil, whisking constantly, until the mixture is smooth and thick. Season with salt and pepper and set aside until needed.

Rinse the frisée; rip into bite-size chunks and dry. Chill until needed.

Place the frisée in a salad bowl, lightly coat with the dressing and toss well. Garnish with the bread crumbs and serve immediately.

VARIATION

Add cooked crumbled bacon or sautéed mushrooms to the final salad.

Wild Greens with Sweet and Sour Tomato Dressing

SERVES 4

2 Tbsp. / 30 mL tomato juice (or ketchup)

1 lemon, juice and zest

1 Tbsp. / 15 mL honey

1 Tbsp. / 15 mL minced garlic

1 tsp. / 5 mL hot sauce (optional)

$^1/_4$ cup / 60 mL olive oil

salt and black pepper to taste

. . . .

1 lb. / 450 g mixed wild greens (such as dandelion, arugula, etc.) or a salad mix

1 recipe Garlic Croutons (page 51)

Place the tomato juice, lemon juice, zest, honey, garlic and hot sauce (if desired) in a mixing bowl. Drizzle in the oil, whisking constantly, until the mixture is smooth and thick. Season with salt and pepper and set aside until needed.

Soak the greens in a bowl of cold water for 10 minutes. Drain the greens and dry. Chill until needed.

Place the greens in a salad bowl, lightly coat with dressing and toss well. Garnish with the croutons and serve immediately.

Mixed Green Salads

Italian Greens with a Roasted Pepper Dressing

1 roasted **red bell pepper**

2 Tbsp. / 30 mL **balsamic vinegar**

1 tsp. / 5 mL **minced garlic**

1 Tbsp. / 15 mL **water**

¹⁄₄ cup / 60 mL **olive oil**

salt and black pepper to taste

. . . .

1 lb. / 450 g **mixed Italian greens**

1 recipe **Parmesan Croutons (page 48)**

Place the roasted pepper, balsamic vinegar, garlic and water in a blender. Process until smooth. With the machine running, add the oil in a slow steady stream until the mixture is smooth and thick. Season well with salt and pepper. Set aside until needed.

Rinse the salad greens; rip into bite-size chunks and dry. Chill until needed.

Place the greens in a salad bowl, coat lightly with the dressing and toss well. Garnish with the croutons and serve immediately.

ROASTING PEPPERS

Roasting intensifies the flavor of sweet peppers and gives them a soft sensual texture. The best method is to place the pepper directly on the burner of a gas stove or barbecue grill and char until the skin is completely black. Alternately, you can broil the peppers under the top element of your oven.

Place the blackened peppers in a bowl and cover with plastic wrap. Rest for at least 5 minutes to allow the internal heat to steam and soften the skins. When the peppers are cool enough to handle, peel off the skin, remove the core and seeds and proceed with the recipe. Roasted pepper makes a great addition to any salad. Simply cut it into strips and toss with the greens and your favorite dressing. Use ¹⁄₄ cup (60 mL) canned or pickled pimento as a quick substitute.

Mesclun with Burnt Honey and Orange Vinaigrette

1 Tbsp. / 15 mL honey
1 orange, juice and zest
1 Tbsp. / 15 mL sherry vinegar
¼ cup / 60 mL olive oil
salt and black pepper to taste
. . . .
1 lb. / 450 g mesclun (or mixed greens)
2 Tbsp. / 30 mL olives, pitted and chopped

Place the honey in a nonstick skillet and cook over medium-high heat until the honey begins to caramelize and turn brown. Add the orange juice quickly (be careful as it will sizzle and splash) and swirl the pan to dissolve the caramel. Return to the heat and cook until all the lumps have disappeared. Add the zest and swirl to mix. Remove from the heat and allow to cool.

Place the orange-honey mixture and vinegar in a mixing bowl. Drizzle in the oil, whisking constantly, until the mixture is smooth and thick. Season with salt and pepper and set aside until needed.

Rinse the greens; rip the larger pieces into bite-size chunks, if necessary, and dry. Chill until needed.

Place the greens in a salad bowl, lightly coat with the dressing and toss well. Garnish with the olives and serve immediately.

Romaine and Olives with Garlic Bread Crumbs

SERVES 4

2 Tbsp. / 30 mL balsamic vinegar

2 Tbsp. / 30 mL chopped olives

1 Tbsp. / 15 mL water

^{1}/$_4$ cup / 60 mL olive oil

salt and black pepper to taste

. . . .

1 large head romaine (or iceberg) lettuce

1 recipe Garlic Bread Crumbs

Place the vinegar, olives and water in a mixing bowl. Drizzle in the oil, whisking constantly, until smooth and thick. Season with salt and pepper and set aside until needed.

Rinse the lettuce; rip into large bite-size chunks, if necessary, and dry. Chill until needed.

Place the lettuce in a salad bowl, lightly coat with the dressing and toss well. Garnish with the bread crumbs and serve immediately.

Garlic Bread Crumbs

MAKES ½ CUP (125 ML)

^{1}/$_2$ cup / 125 mL bread crumbs

2 Tbsp. / 30 mL olive oil

1 Tbsp. / 15 mL minced garlic

salt and black pepper to taste

Place the bread crumbs in a frying pan over medium-high heat. Drizzle with the olive oil, add the garlic and toss well to coat. Season well with salt and pepper and sauté until the crumbs begin to brown. Remove from the heat and place on a plate covered with paper towel to absorb the excess oil. Cool the crumbs to room temperature before using.

Frisée and Beet Tops with Apple Cider Dressing and Hazelnuts

SERVES 4

1 large head frisée (or endive)

2 cups / 500 mL young beet top greens

1 recipe Apple Cider Dressing (page 42)

2 Tbsp. / 30 mL chopped toasted hazelnuts

1 apple, cored and julienned

Rinse the frisée and beet tops; rip the frisée into bite-size chunks. Dry the greens and chill until needed.

Place the greens in a salad bowl, lightly coat with the dressing and toss well. Garnish with hazelnuts and apple and serve immediately.

JULIENNE CUTS

A julienne is slivers of food cut into delicate matchstick strips. Use a sharp knife to cut thin slices of a vegetable or fruit and then cut the slices into thin strips. A good, sharp chef's knife is the best tool, but the French mandoline or Japanese vegetable slicers also work well.

Asian Greens with Pickled Ginger–Avocado Dressing

2 Tbsp. / 30 mL **pickled ginger**

1 Tbsp. / 15 mL **light soy sauce**

1 tsp. / 5 mL **sesame oil**

2 Tbsp. / 30 mL **water**

1 **avocado, peeled, seeded and chopped**

1 **lime, juice and zest**

salt and black pepper to taste

. . . .

1 lb. / 450 g **Asian greens (or salad mix)**

1 Tbsp. / 15 mL **toasted sesame seeds**

Place the pickled ginger, soy sauce, sesame oil, water, avocado, lime juice and zest in a blender. Process until smooth and season well with salt and pepper. Thin with a little water, if necessary, to make a pouring consistency. Chill until needed.

Rinse the greens; rip into bite-size chunks, if necessary, and dry. Chill until needed.

Place the greens in a salad bowl, lightly coat with the dressing and toss well. Sprinkle the sesame seeds on top and serve immediately.

Asian Greens with Spicy Miso Dressing

2 Tbsp. / 30 mL **light miso paste**

1 Tbsp. / 15 mL **light soy sauce**

1 tsp. / 5 mL **hot sauce, or to taste**

2 Tbsp. / 30 mL **water**

1 **lemon, juice and zest**

1 Tbsp. / 15 mL **honey**

salt and black pepper to taste

. . . .

1 lb. / 450 g **Asian greens (or mixed greens)**

1 Tbsp. / 15 mL **toasted sunflower seeds**

Place the miso, soy sauce, hot sauce, water, lemon juice, zest and honey in a mixing bowl. Whisk until smooth and thick. Season with salt and pepper and set aside until needed.

Rinse the greens; rip into bite-size chunks, if necessary, and dry. Chill until needed.

Place the greens in a salad bowl, lightly coat with the dressing and toss well. Garnish with sunflower seeds and serve immediately.

MISO PASTE

Miso is a paste made from cooked, mashed, salted and fermented soybeans. It is often mixed with grains such as rice or barley (and sometimes wheat). The color ranges from cream to dark reddish brown; color and flavor depend on the ratio of soybean to grains, salt content and the fermentation time. The lighter varieties are usually less salty and have a pleasant nutty taste. The darker varieties have a much stronger flavor and can be very salty. Miso paste has a recommended shelf life of six months. It is a great source of high-quality protein and carbohydrates. Miso makes a fantastic instant soup (or stock) when dissolved in hot water.

Spinach and Endive with Cranberry-Pecan Dressing

2 Tbsp. / 30 mL cranberry jelly (or sauce)

1 Tbsp. / 15 mL mustard

2 Tbsp. / 30 mL cranberry juice (or water)

$^1/_4$ cup / 60 mL finely chopped toasted pecans

2 Tbsp. / 30 mL olive oil

salt and black pepper to taste

....

1 lb. / 450 g baby spinach

2 heads Belgian endive

2 Tbsp. / 30 mL dried cranberries

additional whole pecans for garnish

Place the cranberry jelly, mustard, cranberry juice and pecans in a mixing bowl. Drizzle in the olive oil, whisking constantly, until smooth and thick. Season with salt and pepper and set aside until needed.

Rinse the spinach and endive; rip into large bite-size chunks and dry. Chill until needed.

Place the greens in a salad bowl, lightly coat with dressing and toss well. Garnish with the dried cranberries and whole pecans and serve immediately.

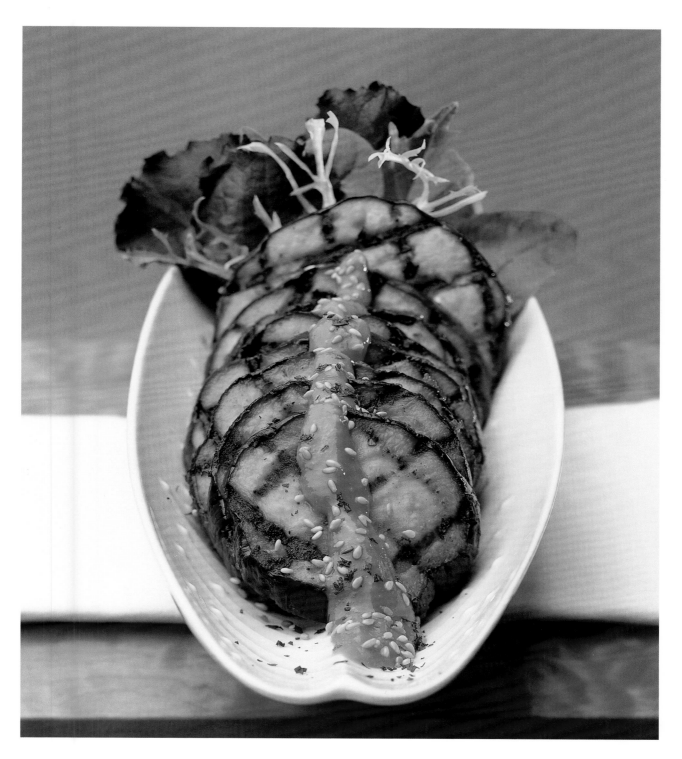

Grilled Eggplant with Miso-Sesame Dressing   p. 75

Mixed Greens and Raisins with Mustard-Rosemary Dressing   p. 66

Tomato and Cucumber with Soy-Mustard Dressing   p. 70

Chinese Egg Noodles with Barbecued Pork and Five-Spice Dressing   p. 87

Crab and Spinach Salad with Soy-Onion Aïoli   p. 126

Mixed Beans with Goat Cheese and Herb Dressing   p. 98

Prawns and Mesclun with Tomato-Horseradish Dressing   p. 106

Penne, Arugula, Prosciutto and Olives with Lemon Vinaigrette   p. 84

Lettuce, Egg and Ham Salad with Thyme Vinaigrette

1 Tbsp. / 15 mL white wine vinegar

1 Tbsp. / 15 mL Dijon mustard

1 Tbsp. / 15 mL minced fresh thyme

1 tsp. / 5 mL minced garlic

1 Tbsp. / 15 mL minced shallots

1 Tbsp. / 15 mL water

$^1/_4$ cup / 60 mL light oil (or nut oil)

salt and black pepper to taste

. . . .

1 large head leaf lettuce

2 hard-boiled eggs, peeled and sliced

$^1/_2$ cup / 125 mL chopped smoked ham

$^1/_4$ cup / 60 mL cubed cheese (Gruyère, hard goat cheese, etc.)

Place the vinegar, mustard, thyme, garlic, shallots and water in a mixing bowl. Drizzle in the oil, whisking constantly, until smooth and thick. Season with salt and pepper and set aside until needed.

Rinse the lettuce; rip into bite-size pieces and dry. Chill until needed.

Place the greens in a salad bowl, lightly coat with the dressing and toss well. Garnish with the eggs, ham and cheese and serve immediately.

PERFECT BOILED EGGS

To make perfect boiled eggs, place the eggs in a small pot, cover with cold water and bring to a boil. Remove from the heat, cover the pot and let sit for 5 minutes for soft yolks and 10 minutes for firm yolks. Remove from the water and rinse eggs under cold running water. Peel and set aside until needed (they can be chilled). Just before serving, slice the egg thinly. Egg yolks contain iron and the whites contain sulfur. Prolonged boiling produces an over-cooked egg; the high temperature causes these two elements to interact — producing a green-gray edge around the yolk and an unpleasant smell.

Mixed Greens and Raisins with Mustard-Rosemary Dressing

1 Tbsp. / 15 mL white wine vinegar

1 Tbsp. / 15 mL mustard

1 Tbsp. / 15 mL minced fresh rosemary

1 Tbsp. / 15 mL water

$^1/_4$ cup / 60 mL olive oil

salt and black pepper to taste

. . . .

1 lb. / 450 g mixed greens

$^1/_4$ cup / 60 mL raisins, soaked in hot water until plump

Place the vinegar, mustard, rosemary and water in a mixing bowl. Drizzle in the oil, whisking constantly, until smooth and thick. Season with salt and pepper and set aside until needed.

Rinse the greens; rip them into bite-size pieces, if necessary, and dry. Chill until needed.

Place the greens in a salad bowl, lightly coat with the dressing and toss well. Drain the raisins, sprinkle them over the salad and serve immediately.

Baby Lettuce and Enoki Mushrooms with Wasabi Vinaigrette

1 Tbsp. / 15 mL **rice vinegar**

1 Tbsp. / 15 mL **light soy sauce**

1 Tbsp. / 15 mL **wasabi paste**

1 tsp. / 5 mL **honey (or sugar)**

1 Tbsp. / 15 mL **water**

$1/4$ cup / 60 mL **light oil**

salt and black pepper to taste

. . . .

1 lb. / 450 g **baby lettuce greens**

1 cup / 250 mL **enoki mushrooms**

1 Tbsp. / 15 mL **toasted sesame seeds**

Place the vinegar, soy sauce, wasabi, honey and water in a mixing bowl. Drizzle in the oil, whisking constantly, until smooth and thick. Season with salt and pepper and set aside until needed.

Rinse the greens; rip them into bite-size pieces, if necessary, and dry. Chill until needed.

Place the greens in a salad bowl, lightly coat with the dressing and toss well. Garnish with the mushrooms, sprinkle the sesame seeds on top and serve immediately.

ENOKI MUSHROOMS

Once rare, enoki mushrooms are increasingly available in markets and grocery stores. Sometimes called the "velvet shank mushroom," enoki mushrooms are mild, nutty and nutritious. In Japan, they are valued for their flavor and for medicinal properties. Extracts from the mushroom have been part of clinical trials and appear to decrease (or limit) the size of cancerous growths and are thought to help boost the immune system. (Similar properties are ascribed to shiitake and oyster mushrooms.) Enokis are often sold in vacuum packs to preserve freshness. Rinse under water and cut off the woody stem. Add them raw to salads or use as a last-minute addition to cooked dishes.

Vegetable Salads

Tomato and Cucumber with Soy-Mustard Dressing

1 tsp. / 5 mL **minced garlic**

1 Tbsp. / 15 mL **rice vinegar**

1 Tbsp. / 15 mL **sweet soy sauce**

1 Tbsp. / 15 mL **mustard**

1 Tbsp. / 15 mL **water**

1 tsp. / 5 mL **sesame oil**

2 Tbsp. / 30 mL **light oil**

salt and black pepper to taste

. . . .

4 medium **tomatoes**

1 small **seedless cucumber**

1 Tbsp. / 15 mL **toasted sesame seeds**

Place the garlic, vinegar, soy sauce, mustard, water and sesame oil in a mixing bowl. Drizzle in the oil, whisking constantly, until smooth and thick. Season with salt and pepper and set aside until needed.

Cut the tomatoes into slices and set aside. Slice the cucumber into rounds. Overlap the cucumber and tomato slices on a platter or plate. Season well with salt and pepper.

Drizzle the dressing over the vegetable slices. Garnish with a sprinkling of sesame seeds.

TOMATOES

Tomatoes are native to South and Central America and are thought to have evolved from something resembling the modern cherry tomato. The Spanish brought the tomato (then called the "love apple") to Europe in the early sixteenth century and it spread outward from there. Tomatoes come in many colors and sizes. White, yellow, orange, purple, green and multi-colored varieties are commonly grown. Look for heirloom varieties from old seed stock or new specialty varieties developed with the characteristics of these flavorful tomatoes. There is a huge world of tomatoes, well worth exploring.

Tomato and Bacon with Mustard-Mayo Dressing

SERVES 4

¹/₄ cup / 60 mL mayonnaise

1 Tbsp. / 15 mL mustard

1 tsp. / 5 mL honey (or maple syrup)

1 Tbsp. / 15 mL white wine vinegar

2 Tbsp. / 30 mL olive oil

salt and black pepper to taste

. . . .

1 lb. / 450 g ripe cherry tomatoes, red or yellow

4 slices bacon, cooked and crumbled (or soy bacon)

2 Tbsp. / 30 mL chopped fresh parsley

Place the mayonnaise, mustard, honey and vinegar in a large salad bowl. Drizzle in the oil, whisking constantly, until smooth and thick. Season with salt and pepper and set aside until needed.

Rinse the tomatoes and drain. Add to the dressing and toss well to coat. Garnish with crumbled bacon and chopped parsley. Serve immediately.

Shredded Carrot with Thai Lime Dressing

1 lime, juice and zest

2 Tbsp. / 30 mL fish sauce (see page 90)

1 Tbsp. / 15 mL minced garlic

1 Tbsp. / 15 mL chopped fresh basil

1 tsp. / 5 mL hot sauce

1 tsp. / 5 mL honey (or sugar)

1/4 cup / 60 mL light oil

salt and black pepper to taste

. . . .

4 cups / 1 L shredded carrot

1 cup / 250 mL bean sprouts

additional sprouts for garnish

whole basil leaves for garnish

2 Tbsp. / 30 mL chopped peanuts (or toasted sesame seeds)

Place the lime juice and zest, fish sauce, garlic, chopped basil, hot sauce and honey in a large salad bowl. Drizzle in the oil, whisking constantly, until smooth and thick. Season with salt and pepper and set aside until needed.

Add the carrot and sprouts to the dressing and toss well to coat. Garnish with the additional sprouts, whole basil leaves and peanuts. Serve immediately.

SHREDDING VEGETABLES

There are several options available for shredding dense vegetables like carrot and jicama. The simplest is a common kitchen grater (the kind often used for cheese). Use the largest hole size, if options are available. Food processors often come with grating disks. These can be great if you are making large quantities (although they are fussy to clean), but they tend to give a fairly short shred. Mandolines, and cheaper Japanese vegetable slicers, often have cutting attachments to create julienne cuts. These are excellent for shredding vegetables and give long, elegant strands — great for presentation.

Grated Jicama and Pumpkin Seeds with Lime and Ginger Dressing

1 lime, juice and zest

1 Tbsp. / 15 mL shredded fresh ginger

1 tsp. / 5 mL honey (or sugar)

$1/4$ cup / 60 mL light oil

salt and black pepper to taste

. . . .

4 cups / 1 L shredded jicama

$1/2$ cup / 125 mL toasted pumpkin seeds

1 Tbsp. / 15 mL chopped cilantro (or fresh parsley)

Place the lime juice, zest, ginger and honey in a large salad bowl. Drizzle in the oil, whisking constantly, until smooth and thick. Season with salt and pepper and set aside until needed.

Add the jicama to the dressing and toss well to coat. Garnish with pumpkin seeds and cilantro and serve immediately.

JICAMA

Jicama, also known as yam bean, is native to Mexico and Central America. It can be eaten raw or cooked and is a good source of vitamin C. The white flesh is crisp and juicy and has been described as a cross between a potato and an apple. Choose tubers that are plump, blemish-free and firm. Peel the thin tough skin just before use.

Grilled Asparagus and Red Pepper with Balsamic Dressing

2 Tbsp. / 30 mL balsamic vinegar

1 Tbsp. / 15 mL chopped fresh sage

1 tsp. / 5 mL minced garlic

2 Tbsp. / 30 mL olive oil

salt and black pepper to taste

. . . .

1 lb. / 450 g asparagus, washed and trimmed

2 red bell peppers, seeded and cut in strips

Preheat the grill to medium-high.

Place the balsamic vinegar, sage and garlic in a large mixing bowl. Drizzle in the oil, whisking constantly, until smooth and thick. Season with salt and pepper. Add the asparagus and red pepper, toss well to coat and allow to sit for at least 5 minutes.

Place the asparagus and peppers on the grill, reserving the dressing. Cook until slightly charred and soft, about 2–3 minutes per side. Remove from the grill and return to the dressing. Toss well to coat all the vegetables. Cool to room temperature or chill before serving.

Grilled Eggplant with Miso-Sesame Dressing

2 Tbsp. / 30 mL light miso (see page 63)

1 Tbsp. / 15 mL light soy sauce

1 tsp. / 5 mL sesame oil

1 lemon, juice and zest

1 Tbsp. / 15 mL honey

2 Tbsp. / 30 mL olive oil

salt and black pepper to taste

· ·

2 medium purple eggplants (or 4 Japanese eggplants)

1 Tbsp. / 15 mL toasted sesame seeds

1 Tbsp. / 15 mL chopped fresh parsley

Preheat the grill to medium-high.

Place the miso, soy sauce, sesame oil, lemon juice, zest and honey in a mixing bowl. Drizzle in the oil, whisking constantly, until smooth and thick. Season with salt and pepper and set aside until needed.

Trim the stems off the eggplants and cut them into thick slices. Add to the dressing and toss well to coat.

Place the eggplant slices on the grill, reserving the dressing. Cook until slightly charred and soft, about 5 minutes per side. Return to the dressing and gently toss to coat. Cool to room temperature or chill before serving. Garnish with the sesame seeds and parsley before serving.

EGGPLANT

Known as aubergine in France and Britain, the eggplant is a native of tropical Asia. It has been cultivated for at least a thousand years (initially in India, where it is known as brinjal) and is now grown all over the world. Large, older specimens may be bitter, particularly when seeds are present. Sprinkling salt on large slices will draw out the moisture and the bitter elements. Wipe the slices clean with a paper towel and proceed with the recipe. Japanese eggplants are slender, light purple vegetables; they have a creamy texture when cooked and are particularly sweet.

Coleslaw with a Grainy Mustard and Herb Dressing

2 Tbsp. / 30 mL mayonnaise

2 Tbsp. / 30 mL grainy mustard

1 Tbsp. / 15 mL white wine vinegar

1 tsp. / 5 mL honey (or sugar)

1 tsp. / 5 mL minced garlic

2 Tbsp. / 30 mL minced fresh herbs
   (parsley, thyme, rosemary, sage, etc.)

2 Tbsp. / 30 mL olive oil

salt and black pepper to taste

. . . .

1 large head cabbage, shredded

2 large carrots, shredded

1 medium red onion, peeled and thinly sliced

$^1/_2$ cup / 125 mL toasted sunflower seeds (or pumpkin seeds)

Place the mayonnaise, mustard, vinegar, honey, garlic and herbs in a large mixing bowl. Drizzle in the oil, whisking constantly, until smooth and thick. Season with salt and pepper and set aside until needed.

Add the cabbage, carrots and onion to the dressing and toss well to mix. Chill until needed. Toss the coleslaw again and garnish with the sunflower seeds just before serving. Serve immediately for a crunchy salad. Allowing the coleslaw to sit will draw moisture from the cabbage and make a softer-textured salad.

Coleslaw with Curried Peanut Dressing

SERVES 4

2 Tbsp. / 30 mL mayonnaise

2 Tbsp. / 30 mL peanut butter

1 Tbsp. / 15 mL curry paste

1 Tbsp. / 15 mL white wine vinegar

1 Tbsp. / 15 mL hot water

1 tsp. / 5 mL sugar

1 Tbsp. / 15 mL minced ginger

2 Tbsp. / 30 mL chopped cilantro

salt and black pepper to taste

. . . .

1 head cabbage, shredded

2 medium carrots, shredded

1 red onion, peeled and thinly sliced

1/2 cup / 125 mL dry-roasted peanuts, chopped

Place the mayonnaise, peanut butter, curry paste, vinegar, hot water, sugar, ginger and cilantro in a large mixing bowl. Whisk until smooth, season with salt and pepper and refrigerate until needed.

Add the cabbage, carrots and onion to the dressing and toss well to mix. Chill until needed. Toss the coleslaw again and garnish with chopped peanuts just before serving.

Sweet Corn and Cauliflower in Curry Vinaigrette

SERVES 4

1 Tbsp. / 15 mL minced garlic

1 Tbsp. / 15 mL minced ginger

2 Tbsp. / 30 mL white wine vinegar

1 tsp. / 5 mL curry paste

1 tsp. / 5 mL honey

1 lime, juice and zest

$^1/_4$ cup / 60 mL light oil

salt and black pepper to taste

. . . .

2 cups / 500 mL cooked corn kernels

4 cups / 1 L cooked cauliflower florets

1 Tbsp. / 15 mL chopped cilantro

Place the garlic, ginger, vinegar, curry paste, honey, lime juice and zest in a large mixing bowl. Drizzle in the oil, whisking constantly, until smooth and thick. Season with salt and pepper and set aside until needed.

Add the corn and cauliflower to the dressing and toss to coat. Garnish with chopped cilantro and serve immediately.

Roasted Squash and Mushrooms with Maple-Mustard Dressing

2 Tbsp. / 30 mL grainy mustard

1 Tbsp. / 15 mL maple syrup

1 tsp. / 5 mL hot sauce

1 Tbsp. / 15 mL water

$^1/_4$ cup / 60 mL olive oil

salt and black pepper to taste

. . . .

4 cups / 1 L cubed, peeled squash

4 cups / 1 L quartered mushrooms

1 Tbsp. / 15 mL minced garlic

2 Tbsp. / 30 mL olive oil

salt and black pepper to taste

1 Tbsp. / 15 mL chopped fresh parsley

Preheat the oven to 400°F / 200°C.

Place the mustard, maple syrup, hot sauce and water in a large mixing bowl. Drizzle in the $^1/_4$ cup /60 mL oil, whisking constantly, until smooth and thick. Season with salt and pepper and set aside until needed.

Place the squash, mushrooms and garlic in a heavy roasting pan. Drizzle in the 2 Tbsp. /30 mL oil and toss well to coat. Season well with salt and pepper. Place in the oven and roast until the squash is easily pierced with a fork, about 20 minutes.

Remove the vegetables from the oven and add them to the dressing, scraping the pan if necessary. Toss well to coat and cool to room temperature. Garnish with parsley just before serving.

Pasta & Noodle Salads

Macaroni and Cherry Tomatoes with Sun-Dried Tomato Vinaigrette

SERVES 4–6

FOR THE DRESSING

1 Tbsp. / 15 mL minced sun-dried tomatoes

1 tsp. / 5 mL minced garlic

1 Tbsp. / 15 mL white balsamic vinegar

1 Tbsp. / 15 mL minced fresh basil

1 lemon, juice only

2 Tbsp. / 30 mL olive oil

salt and black pepper to taste

Place the tomato, garlic, vinegar, basil and lemon juice in a large salad bowl. Drizzle in the oil, whisking constantly, until smooth and thick. Season with salt and pepper and set aside until needed.

. . . .

FOR THE PASTA

6 cups / 1.5 L water

1 tsp. / 5 mL salt

2 cups / 500 mL macaroni

1 tsp. / 5 mL olive oil

additional olive oil for drizzling

1 lb. / 450 g cherry tomatoes

2 Tbsp. / 30 mL chopped basil

1 Tbsp. / 15 mL grated Parmesan cheese

Bring the water and salt to a rolling boil and stir in the macaroni and oil. Bring back to a boil and cook until al dente, about 6–7 minutes. If it foams, reduce the heat to medium-high. Drain and shake the pasta free of excess water. Drizzle with a little olive oil and toss well. Transfer to a baking sheet and spread out evenly. Cool to room temperature and toss lightly to separate.

Add the cooled macaroni and cherry tomatoes to the dressing and toss well to coat. Garnish with the basil and cheese. Serve at room temperature.

PROSCIUTTO

Prosciutto is Italian ham that is salt-cured and unsmoked. The best prosciutto comes from the Parma region, where the ham is particularly sweet. In regions that produce fine hard cheeses, the leftover whey is fed to the local pigs. The nutrient and sugar-rich feed produces hams that are sweet, well marbled and luscious. Prosciutto-like hams are made in various parts of the world, with varying degrees of quality. Other good examples are Serrano and Jambon de Bayonne. Prosciutto is widely available in Italian markets, delicatessens and fine grocery stores.

Fusilli, Asparagus and Ham with Sherry Dressing

SERVES 4–6

FOR THE DRESSING

1 Tbsp. / 15 mL sherry vinegar

1 tsp. / 5 mL minced garlic

1 tsp. / 5 mL minced fresh thyme

1 Tbsp. / 15 mL grainy mustard

2 Tbsp. / 30 mL mayonnaise

2 Tbsp. / 30 mL olive oil

salt and black pepper to taste

Place the vinegar, garlic, thyme, mustard and mayonnaise in a large salad bowl. Drizzle in the oil, whisking constantly, until smooth and thick. Season with salt and pepper and set aside until needed.

. . . .

FOR THE SALAD

6 cups / 1.5 L water

1 tsp. / 5 mL salt

2 cups / 500 mL fusilli

1 tsp. / 5 mL olive oil

1 lb. / 450 g asparagus, trimmed and sliced

additional olive oil for drizzling

$^1/_2$ cup / 125 mL cubed ham

1 tsp. / 5 mL minced fresh thyme

Bring the water and salt to a rolling boil and stir in the fusilli and oil. Bring back to a boil and cook for 4 minutes. If it foams, reduce the heat to medium-high. Add the asparagus to the pan and cook until the pasta is al dente and the asparagus is tender, about 3 minutes. Drain and shake the pasta and asparagus free of excess water. Drizzle with a little oil and toss well. Transfer to a baking sheet and spread out evenly. Cool to room temperature and toss lightly to separate.

Add the cooled fusilli and asparagus to the dressing. Add the ham and toss well to coat. Garnish with the thyme and serve at room temperature.

Penne, Arugula, Prosciutto and Olives with Lemon Vinaigrette

SERVES 4–6

FOR THE DRESSING

1 lemon, juice and zest

1 Tbsp. / 15 mL Dijon mustard

1 tsp. / 5 mL minced garlic

1 tsp. / 5 mL water

4 Tbsp. / 60 mL olive oil

salt and black pepper to taste

Place the lemon juice, zest, mustard, garlic and water in a large salad bowl. Drizzle in the oil, whisking constantly, until smooth and thick. Season with salt and pepper and set aside until needed.

. . . .

FOR THE PASTA

6 cups / 1.5 L water

1 tsp. / 5 mL salt

2 cups / 500 mL penne

1 tsp. / 5 mL olive oil

additional olive oil for drizzling

2 cups / 500 mL arugula leaves

2 oz. / 60 g shredded prosciutto

$^1/_2$ cup / 125 mL whole olives

additional prosciutto and olives for garnish

Bring the water and salt to a rolling boil and stir in the penne and oil. Bring back to a boil and cook until al dente, about 7–8 minutes. If it foams, reduce the heat to medium-high. Drain and shake the pasta free of excess water. Drizzle with a little oil and toss well. Transfer to a baking sheet and spread out evenly. Cool to room temperature and toss lightly to separate.

Add the cooled penne, arugula, prosciutto and olives to the dressing and toss well to mix. Garnish with a sprinkling of extra shredded prosciutto and olives. Serve at room temperature.

Bow Pasta and Spinach with
Creamy Smoked Salmon Dressing

SERVE 4–6

FOR THE DRESSING

1 lemon, juice and zest

2 Tbsp. / 30 mL sour cream

2 Tbsp. / 30 mL mayonnaise

2 Tbsp. / 30 mL water

1/4 cup / 60 mL chopped smoked salmon

1 tsp. / 5 mL capers

2 Tbsp. / 30 mL olive oil

salt and black pepper to taste

Place the lemon juice, zest, sour cream, mayonnaise, water, smoked salmon, capers and oil in a blender. Process until smooth and season lightly with salt and well with pepper. Thin with a little water, if necessary, to make a pouring consistency. Chill until needed.

. . . .

FOR THE PASTA

6 cups / 1.5 L water

1 tsp. / 5 mL salt

2 cups / 500 mL bow pasta

1 tsp. / 5 mL olive oil

additional olive for drizzling

4 cups / 1 L washed baby spinach leaves

1/4 cup / 60 mL shredded smoked salmon

1 Tbsp. / 15 mL capers

Bring the water and salt to a rolling boil and stir in the pasta and oil. Bring back to a boil and cook until al dente, about 7–8 minutes. If it foams, reduce the heat to medium-high. Drain and shake the pasta free of excess water. Drizzle with a little oil and toss well. Transfer to a baking sheet and spread out evenly. Cool to room temperature and toss lightly to separate.

Place the cooked pasta and spinach in a large salad bowl. Add the dressing and toss well to coat. Sprinkle with the salmon and capers and serve immediately.

Shell Pasta and Shaved Parmesan with Creamy Artichoke Dressing

SERVES 4–6

FOR THE DRESSING

1 lemon, juice and zest

1 cup / 250 mL cooked artichokes

2 Tbsp. / 30 mL water

2 Tbsp. / 30 mL olive oil

salt and black pepper to taste

Place the lemon juice, zest, artichokes, water and oil in a blender. Process until smooth and season with salt and pepper. Thin with a little water, if necessary, to make a pouring consistency. Set aside until needed.

. . . .

FOR THE PASTA

6 cups / 1.5 L water

1 tsp. / 5 mL salt

2 cups / 500 mL shell pasta

1 tsp. / 5 mL olive oil

additional olive oil for drizzling

$^1/_4$ cup / 60 mL sliced cooked artichokes

$^1/_4$ cup / 60 mL shaved Parmesan cheese

1 Tbsp. / 15 mL chopped fresh Italian parsley

Bring the water and salt to a rolling boil and stir in the pasta and oil. Bring back to a boil and cook until al dente, about 7–8 minutes. If it foams, reduce the heat to medium-high. Drain and shake the pasta free of excess water. Drizzle with a little oil and toss well. Transfer to a baking sheet and spread out evenly. Cool to room temperature and toss lightly to separate.

Place the cooked pasta in a large salad bowl and add the dressing. Toss well to coat. Sprinkle with the artichoke slices, Parmesan cheese and parsley.

ARTICHOKES

The globe artichoke is native to the Mediterranean and was valued as a food plant by the ancient Romans. The plant is a member of the thistle family and the part we eat is the base of the flower. The tough outer leaves are removed, leaving the tender core beneath. Cook the raw artichoke in plenty of boiling salted water (1 tsp. / 5 mL salt per 4 cups / 1 L water) along with the juice of half a lemon. The acidity of the lemon (or 1 Tbsp. / 15 mL vinegar) will stop the artichoke from oxidizing and turning an unappetizing gray. Canned artichokes are readily available and make a good substitute.

Chinese Egg Noodles with Barbecued Pork and Five-Spice Dressing

FOR THE DRESSING

1 Tbsp. / 15 mL **light soy sauce**

1 Tbsp. / 15 mL **honey**

1 Tbsp. / 15 mL **rice vinegar**

1 tsp. / 5 mL **five-spice powder**

1 tsp. / 5 mL **sesame oil**

2 Tbsp. / 30 mL **water**

2 Tbsp. / 30 mL **light oil**

salt and black pepper to taste

Place the soy sauce, honey, vinegar, five-spice powder, sesame oil and water in a large salad bowl. Drizzle in the oil, whisking constantly, until smooth and thick. Season with salt and pepper and set aside until needed.

. . . .

FOR THE NOODLES

8 cups / 2 L **water**

1 tsp. / 5 mL **salt**

1 lb. / 450 g **fresh Chinese egg noodles (chow mein)**

1 tsp. / 5 mL **light oil**

additional light oil for drizzling

2 cups / 500 mL **shredded head lettuce (iceberg, romaine, etc.)**

1 cup / 250 mL **shredded Chinese barbecued pork**

1 cup / 250 mL **bean sprouts**

1 **green onion, thinly sliced**

1 Tbsp. / 15 mL **toasted sesame seeds**

Bring the water and salt to a rolling boil and stir in the noodles and oil. Bring back to a boil and cook until al dente, about 3–4 minutes. If it foams, reduce the heat to medium-high. Drain and shake free of excess water. Drizzle with a little oil and toss the noodles well. Transfer to a baking sheet and spread out evenly (see page 88). Cool to room temperature and toss lightly to separate.

Add the cooled noodles, lettuce, pork and bean sprouts to the dressing. Toss well to mix and sprinkle with the green onion and sesame seeds. Serve immediately.

VARIATIONS

Substitute ½ lb. (225 g) dried noodles for 1 lb (450 g) fresh noodles. Replace the barbecued pork with ham, cooked chicken or tofu.

FIVE-SPICE POWDER

Traditional in Chinese cookery, five-spice powder is a blend of aromatic spices. There are many combinations but a common blend includes star anise, cinnamon, Szechwan pepper, fennel and ginger. It is very fragrant and adds a wonderful spice note to many types of dishes. It is available in Asian markets and is found increasingly in mainstream grocery stores.

Rice Noodles with Mint-Chili Vinaigrette

FOR THE VINAIGRETTE

1 lime, juice and zest

1 Tbsp. / 15 mL brown sugar

2 Tbsp. / 30 mL fish sauce

1 Tbsp. / 15 mL chopped fresh mint

1 tsp. / 5 mL chili paste (or hot sauce) to taste

2 Tbsp. / 30 mL light oil

salt and black pepper to taste

Place the lime juice and zest, sugar, fish sauce, chopped mint and chili paste in a large salad bowl. Drizzle in the oil, whisking constantly, until smooth and thick. Season with salt and pepper and set aside until needed.

. . . .

FOR THE NOODLES

8 cups / 2 L water

1 tsp. / 5 mL salt

1 lb. / 455 g thin fresh rice noodles

light oil for drizzling

1 cup / 250 mL shredded lettuce

1 cup / 250 mL bean sprouts

1 cup / 250 mL shredded peeled carrot

lime wedges for garnish

whole mint leaves for garnish

Bring the water and salt to a rolling boil and stir in the noodles. Bring back to a boil and cook until the noodles are soft and slightly puffy, about 1 minute. Drain and shake off excess water. Drizzle with a little oil and toss well. Transfer to a baking sheet and spread out evenly. Cool to room temperature and toss lightly to separate.

Add the cooled noodles, lettuce, bean sprouts and carrot to the dressing. Toss well to coat and garnish with the lime wedges and whole mint leaves. Serve immediately.

RICE NOODLES

Many styles of rice noodles are available: flat ribbons (similar to fettucini), round noodles (similar to spaghetti) and thin strands (similar to vermicelli). Fresh rice noodles are ready to eat and need only be heated through in water to loosen them up. Dried noodles take slightly longer, 2–3 minutes, and benefit from presoaking in water until soft and pliable, about 15 minutes. You can cut the noodles with a pair of scissors to make the pieces more manageable. Use fresh noodles within 1–2 days of purchase. Dried noodles will last indefinitely. You can substitute ½ lb. (225 g) dried noodles for 1 lb. (450 g) fresh noodles.

Noodles and Smoked Chicken with Hoisin Vinaigrette

SERVES 4–6

FOR THE VINAIGRETTE

1 Tbsp. / 15 mL rice vinegar

2 Tbsp. / 30 mL hoisin sauce

1 Tbsp. / 15 mL chopped cilantro

1 tsp. / 5 mL sesame oil

1 tsp. / 5 mL hot sauce

2 Tbsp. / 30 mL water

2 Tbsp. / 30 mL light oil

salt and black pepper to taste

Place the vinegar, hoisin sauce, cilantro, sesame oil, hot sauce and water in a large salad bowl. Drizzle in the oil, whisking constantly, until smooth and thick. Season with salt and pepper and set aside until needed.

. . . .

FOR THE NOODLES

8 cups / 2 L water

1 tsp. / 5 mL salt

1 lb. / 450 g fresh Shanghai (round) noodles

1 tsp. / 5 mL light oil

additional light oil for drizzling

1 cup / 250 mL shredded smoked chicken

1 cup / 250 mL shredded seedless cucumber

1 cup / 250 mL finely diced firm tofu

1 green onion, thinly sliced

1 Tbsp. / 15 mL toasted sesame seeds

Bring the water and salt to a rolling boil and stir in the noodles and oil. Bring back to a boil and cook until the noodles are soft and slightly puffy, about 2–3 minutes. Drain and shake free of excess water. Drizzle with a little oil and toss well. Transfer to a baking sheet and spread out evenly (see page 88). Cool to room temperature and toss lightly to separate.

Add the cooled noodles, chicken, cucumber and tofu to the dressing. Toss well to coat and garnish with the green onion and sesame seeds. Serve immediately.

ASIAN WHEAT NOODLES
Fresh Asian wheat noodles are now widely available in grocery stores. Mein noodles (often called chow mein) are long flat ribbons of egg noodles. Shanghai noodles are long round strands of wheat pasta, similar to thick spaghetti. The noodles cook very quickly and will rapidly overcook if left too long on the heat. Use fresh noodles within 2–3 days of purchase, or freeze for up to 2 weeks. Dried wheat noodles will last indefinitely. You can substitute ½ lb. (225 g) dried noodles for 1 lb. (450 g) fresh noodles.

Rice Noodles with Curried Coconut Dressing

SERVES 4–6

FOR THE DRESSING

1 lime, juice and zest

$^1/_4$ cup / 60 mL coconut milk

1 Tbsp. / 15 mL fish sauce

1 Tbsp. / 15 mL sweet soy sauce

1 Tbsp. / 15 mL chopped fresh basil

1 tsp. / 5 mL curry paste

salt and black pepper to taste

Place the lime juice, zest, coconut milk, fish sauce, soy sauce, chopped basil and curry paste in a large salad bowl. Whisk until smooth. Season with salt and pepper and set aside until needed.

. . . .

FOR THE NOODLES

8 cups / 2 L water

1 tsp. / 5 mL salt

1 lb. / 450 g thick fresh rice noodles (see page 88)

1 tsp. / 5 mL light oil

additional light oil for drizzling

1 cup / 250 mL bean sprouts

1 cup / 250 mL shredded, peeled carrot

1 cup / 250 mL shredded green cabbage

$^1/_4$ cup / 60 mL chopped roasted peanuts

lime wedges for garnish

whole basil leaves for garnish

Bring the water and salt to a rolling boil and stir in the rice noodles and 1 tsp. / 5 mL oil. Bring back to a boil and cook until the noodles are soft and slightly puffy, about 2–3 minutes. Drain the noodles and shake them free of excess water. Drizzle with a little oil and toss the noodles well. Transfer to a baking sheet and spread out evenly (see page 88). Cool to room temperature and toss lightly to separate.

Add the cooled noodles, bean sprouts, carrot and cabbage to the dressing. Toss well to coat. Sprinkle with the peanuts, garnish with lime wedges and basil leaves and serve immediately.

FISH SAUCE

Fish sauce is an important ingredient in many Asian cuisines. The sauce is made by fermenting fish and salt to produce a pungent amber liquid, full of protein and vitamins. It is used as a condiment or a flavoring in many dishes. Known as *nam pla* in Thailand and *nuoc nam* in Vietnam, fish sauce is available in Asian markets and grocery stores and will keep indefinitely.

Soba Noodles with Cucumber, Avocado and Nori

SERVES 4–6

FOR THE DRESSING

1 lemon, juice and zest

1 Tbsp. / 15 mL light soy sauce

1 tsp. / 5 mL honey

1 Tbsp. / 15 mL wasabi (or mustard)

2 Tbsp. / 30 mL light oil

salt and black pepper to taste

Place the lemon juice, zest, soy sauce, honey and wasabi in a large salad bowl. Drizzle in the 2 Tbsp. (30 mL) oil, whisking constantly, until smooth and thick. Season with salt and pepper and set aside until needed.

. . . .

FOR THE NOODLES

8 cups / 2 L water

1 tsp. / 5 mL salt

1 lb. / 450 g fresh soba noodles

1 tsp. / 5 mL light oil

additional light oil for drizzling

1 small hot house cucumber, shredded

1 ripe avocado, pitted, peeled and cut in strips

1 cup / 250 mL shredded lettuce

1 sheet nori, cut in thin strips (see page 52)

1 Tbsp. / 15 mL toasted sesame seeds

Bring the water and salt to a rolling boil and stir in the soba noodles and 1 tsp. / 5 mL oil. Bring back to a boil and cook until the noodles are soft and slightly puffy, about 2–3 minutes. Drain and shake free of excess water. Drizzle with a little oil and toss well. Transfer to a baking sheet and spread out evenly (you can cut the noodles with a pair of scissors to make the pieces more manageable). Cool to room temperature and toss lightly to separate.

Add the cooled noodles, cucumber, avocado and lettuce to the dressing. Toss well to coat and garnish with the nori and sesame seeds. Serve immediately.

SOBA NOODLES

Originally a specialty of northern Japan, soba noodles are made from buckwheat flour (usually with a percentage of wheat flour). The noodles are available fresh, dried or frozen in many Asian markets and in health food stores. Soba is a good source of dietary fiber, protein, vitamins and minerals. It contains significant amounts of rutin, a bioflavinoid that is linked to lowering blood pressure. You can substitute ½ lb. (225 g) dried noodles for 1 lb. (450 g) fresh.

Bean & Grain Salads

Cannellini Beans with Olive Oil and Balsamic Vinegar

2 cups / 500 mL **dried cannellini beans**

1 tsp. / 5 mL **minced garlic**

1 Tbsp. / 15 mL **balsamic vinegar**

$^1/_4$ cup / 60 mL **olive oil**

salt and black pepper to taste

$^1/_4$ cup / 60 mL **chopped olives**

1 medium **tomato, seeded and diced**

Place the beans in a medium pot and cover with 8 cups / 2 L of cold water. Soak for at least 2 hours, preferably overnight. Drain the beans and add 8 cups / 2 L fresh cold water.

Place the pot over high heat and bring the beans to a boil. Skim off any scum that floats to the surface. Reduce the heat to a simmer and cook until the beans are tender but still hold their shape, about 1 hour.

Drain the beans and set aside to cool to handling temperature. While the beans are still slightly warm, add the garlic, vinegar and olive oil. Toss well to coat and season well with salt and pepper. Garnish with the olives and diced tomatoes. Serve at room temperature.

BEAN TIPS

Buy organic beans if possible. The skin should appear plump, without wrinkles (which indicate older beans). Soak the beans in fresh cold water; hot water will yield beans that never soften properly and will produce more gas. Do not salt the cooking water as salt will prevent the beans from softening. All beans cook at different rates, so start testing after 30 minutes. It may take anywhere from 50 minutes to 3 hours to cook some beans properly, depending on the age and type of bean. Overcooked beans will split and eventually turn to mush. These beans can be salvaged if you turn them into puréed soup or mashed bean purée.

White Beans with Ham, Caramelized Onions and Orange Vinaigrette

2 cups / 500 mL dried white beans

. . . .

1 orange, juice and zest

1 tsp. / 5 mL minced garlic

1 Tbsp. / 15 mL sherry vinegar

1 Tbsp. / 15 mL mustard

1 tsp. / 5 mL honey

1/4 cup / 60 mL olive oil

salt and black pepper to taste

. . . .

1 recipe Caramelized Onions

1 cup / 250 mL diced ham

1/4 cup / 60 mL toasted pine nuts

Place the beans in a medium pot and cover with 8 cups / 2 L cold water. Allow to soak for at least 2 hours, preferably overnight. Drain the beans and add 8 cups / 2 L fresh cold water.

Place the pot over high heat and bring the mixture to a boil. Skim off any scum that floats to the surface. Reduce the heat to a simmer and cook until the beans are tender but still hold their shape, about 1 hour (see page 94).

Place the orange juice, zest, garlic, vinegar, mustard and honey in a large salad bowl. Drizzle in the oil, whisking constantly, until smooth and thick. Season with salt and pepper and set aside until needed.

While the drained beans are still slightly warm, add them to the dressing. Add the caramelized onions and ham and toss well to coat. Taste for seasoning and adjust with salt and pepper. Garnish with the pine nuts and serve at room temperature.

Caramelized Onions

MAKES ABOUT 1 CUP (250 mL)

1 Tbsp. / 15 mL olive oil

2 medium onions, peeled and diced

1 tsp. / 5 mL honey

1/4 cup / 60 mL white wine

1 tsp. / 5 mL sherry vinegar

1 tsp. / 5 mL chopped thyme

salt and black pepper to taste

Place the oil and diced onion in a nonstick skillet over medium-high heat. Sauté until the onions begin to brown, about 3–4 minutes. Add the honey, stirring well. When the mixture begins to caramelize, add the wine, vinegar and thyme. Season well with salt and pepper and stir well. Cook until all the liquid has evaporated, about 5–6 minutes. Remove from the heat and set aside to cool.

Runner Beans with Herb Vinaigrette

8 cups / 2 L water

1 Tbsp. / 15 mL salt

1 lb. / 450 g runner beans, stems removed

. . . .

1 tsp. / 5 mL minced garlic

1 Tbsp. / 15 mL white wine vinegar

2 Tbsp. / 30 mL chopped fresh herbs (thyme, savory,
  marjoram, sage, etc)

1 Tbsp. / 15 mL water

1/4 cup / 60 mL olive oil

salt and black pepper to taste

Bring the water and salt to a rolling boil and add the runner beans.
Cook until the beans are tender, about 6–7 minutes. Remove from
the heat, drain and place in a bowl of ice water. When the beans are
chilled, drain and set aside.

Place the garlic, vinegar, herbs and water in a salad bowl. Drizzle
in the oil, whisking constantly, until smooth and thick. Season
with salt and pepper and set aside until needed.

Add the cooled beans to the dressing and toss well to mix. Serve
at room temperature.

RUNNER BEANS

Runner beans are another food originating
in Central and South America. Archeological
evidence in Peru dates the cultivation of
beans back to at least 5000 BC. You can
now find runner beans in shades of green,
yellow, purple and mottled variations. Buy
fresh beans that are plump and free of
blemishes. Remove the stem and try to peel
off any "strings" that line both sides of the
bean pod. Cooking beans in boiling well-
salted water helps to set a vivid color and
enhances the flavor.

Curried Potato and Yam   p. 130

Crusted Oysters with Sweet Chili Dressing over Coleslaw   p. 127

Maple-Glazed Duck Breast over Greens and Wild Mushrooms   p. 122

Tortilla Roll with Tuna Salad, Shredded Lettuce and Cheddar   p. 143

Yellow Wax Beans with a Spicy Garlic Dressing

SERVES 4

8 cups / 2 L water
1 Tbsp. / 15 mL salt
1 lb. / 450 g yellow wax beans, stems removed
. . . .
1 tsp. / 5 mL minced garlic
1 Tbsp. / 15 mL rice vinegar
1 Tbsp. / 15 mL chopped cilantro
1 tsp. / 5 mL chili paste (or to taste)
1 Tbsp. / 15 mL water
$^{1}/_{4}$ cup / 60 mL light oil
salt and black pepper to taste
1 Tbsp. / 15 mL toasted sesame seeds

Bring the water and salt to a rolling boil and add the wax beans. Cook until the beans are tender, about 6–7 minutes. Remove from the heat, drain and place in a bowl of ice water. When the beans are chilled, drain and set aside.

Place the garlic, vinegar, cilantro, chili paste and water in a salad bowl. Drizzle in the oil, whisking constantly, until smooth and thick. Season with salt and pepper.

Add the cooled beans to the dressing and toss well to mix. Taste for seasoning and adjust with salt and pepper. Sprinkle with sesame seeds and serve at room temperature.

Mixed Beans with Goat Cheese and Herb Dressing

2 cups / 500 mL **dried beans (navy, cannellini, etc.)**

. . . .

4 cups / 1 L **water**

1 Tbsp. / 15 mL **salt**

2 cups / 1L **runner beans, stems removed**

. . . .

1 tsp. / 5 mL **minced garlic**

1 Tbsp. / 15 mL **white wine vinegar**

1 Tbsp. / 15 mL **minced fresh rosemary**

2 Tbsp. / 30 mL **soft goat cheese**

1 Tbsp. / 15 mL **water**

¼ cup / 60 mL **olive oil**

salt and black pepper to taste

Place the dried beans in a medium pot and cover with 8 cups / 2 L cold water. Allow to soak for at least 2 hours, preferably overnight. Drain the beans and add 8 cups / 2 L fresh cold water.

Place the pot over high heat and bring the mixture to a boil. Skim off any scum that floats to the surface. Reduce the heat to a simmer and cook until the beans are tender but still hold their shape, about 1 hour (see page 94).

Bring the 4 cups / 1 L water and salt to a rolling boil and add the runner beans. Cook until the beans are tender, about 6–7 minutes. Remove from the heat, drain and place in a bowl of ice water. When the beans are chilled, drain and set aside.

Place the garlic, vinegar, rosemary, goat cheese and the 1 Tbsp. /15 mL water in a blender and process until smooth. With the blender running, add the oil in a steady stream. Season well with salt and pepper.

Place the cooled beans in a salad bowl and add the dressing. Toss well to mix. Taste for seasoning and adjust with salt and pepper. Serve at room temperature.

Wild Rice and Mushrooms with Honey-Lemon Dressing

2 cups / 500 mL wild rice

6 cups / 1.5 L water

1 Tbsp. / 15 mL salt

· ·

1 tsp. / 5 mL minced ginger

1 tsp. / 5 mL minced garlic

1 lemon, juice and zest

1 Tbsp. / 15 mL honey

1 Tbsp. / 15 mL water

$^1/_4$ cup / 60 mL olive oil

salt and black pepper to taste

· ·

2 cups / 500 mL diced button mushrooms (raw or sautéed)

$^1/_4$ cup / 60 mL dried cranberries (or blueberries)

WILD RICE

A northern native of North America, wild rice is actually the seed of a freshwater aquatic grass. Wild rice has been harvested for thousands of years by First Nations peoples. Much of today's crop is cultivated. It is a good source of protein, amino acids and vitamin B complexes. Soaking the grain shortens the cooking time. Cook until the grains are soft and completely split.

Place the rice in a medium-small pot, add water to cover and soak for at least 1 hour. Drain the rice and return to the pot. Add the 6 cups / 1.5 L water and salt. Bring to a boil over high heat, reduce to a simmer and cook until the grains are soft and split, about 30–45 minutes. Remove from the heat and cool in the liquid. Strain the rice and set aside.

Place the ginger, garlic, lemon juice, zest, honey and water in a large salad bowl. Drizzle in the oil, whisking constantly, until smooth and thick. Season with salt and pepper.

Add the cooled wild rice and mushrooms to the dressing and toss well to mix. Taste for seasoning and adjust with salt and pepper. Garnish with the cranberries and serve at room temperature.

Bean Sprouts, Vegetables and Couscous with Cumin-Lime Vinaigrette

1 lime, juice and zest

1 tsp. / 5 mL ground cumin

1 Tbsp. / 15 mL mustard

1 tsp. / 5 mL honey

1 Tbsp. / 15 mL water

4 Tbsp. / 60 mL olive oil

salt and black pepper to taste

. . . .

2 cups / 500 mL quick-cooking couscous

2 cups / 500 mL boiling stock (or water)

1 tsp. / 5 mL salt

. . . .

2 cups / 500 mL bean sprouts

1 cup / 250 mL shredded peeled carrot

1 cup / 250 mL shredded cabbage

1 cup / 250 mL shredded yam

$^1/_4$ cup / 60 mL toasted sunflower seeds (see page 46)

1 Tbsp. / 15 mL chopped cilantro

Place the lime juice, zest, cumin, mustard, honey and water in a large salad bowl. Drizzle in the oil, whisking constantly, until smooth and thick. Season with salt and pepper and set aside until needed.

Place the couscous, stock, and salt in a medium heat-proof bowl. Cover with plastic wrap and set aside for at least 15 minutes. Fluff with a fork to separate the grains.

Add the coucous, bean sprouts, carrot, cabbage and yam to the dressing and toss well to mix. Garnish with the sunflower seeds and cilantro and serve immediately.

Couscous Salad with Port-Marinated Dried Fruit

$^1/_4$ cup / 60 mL raisins

$^1/_4$ cup / 60 mL dried cranberries

$^1/_4$ cup / 60 mL diced dried apricots

$^1/_4$ cup / 60 mL diced dried apple

2 Tbsp. / 30 mL port (or red wine or orange marmalade)

$^1/_2$ cup / 125 mL boiling water

. . . .

2 cups / 500 mL quick-cooking (or Israeli-style) couscous

2 cups / 500 mL boiling stock (or water)

1 tsp. / 5 mL salt

1 Tbsp. / 15 mL minced fresh ginger

. . . .

2 Tbsp. / 30 mL white wine vinegar

$^1/_4$ cup / 60 mL olive oil

1 Tbsp. / 15 mL chopped fresh mint

$^1/_4$ cup / 60 mL toasted sliced almonds

salt and black pepper to taste

additional almonds and mint for garnish

Place the raisins, cranberries, apricots and apple in a strainer, rinse under running water and drain.

Place the dried fruit, port and boiling water in a small heat-proof bowl. Cover with plastic wrap and set aside for at least 1 hour.

Place the couscous, stock, salt and ginger in a medium heat-proof bowl. Cover with plastic wrap and set aside for at least 15 minutes. Fluff with a fork to separate the grains.

Place the vinegar, oil, mint and almonds in a large salad bowl. Stir to mix and add the couscous and fruit mixes. Toss well to mix, and season with salt and pepper. Garnish with additional mint and almonds and serve at room temperature.

Wheat Berries and Squash with Maple–Sunflower Seed Dressing

SERVES 4–6

6 cups / 1.5 L water
1 tsp. / 5 mL salt
2 cups / 500 mL wheat berries
. . . .
2 cups / 500 mL squash, cut into $^1/_2$-inch (1-cm) dice
1 Tbsp. / 15 mL minced garlic
2 Tbsp. / 30 mL olive oil
salt and black pepper to taste
. . . .
1 Tbsp. / 15 mL apple cider vinegar
1 tsp. / 5 mL minced garlic
$^1/_2$ cup / 125 mL toasted sunflower seeds
2 Tbsp / 30 mL apple juice (or water)
1 Tbsp. / 15 mL maple syrup
salt and black pepper to taste
additional toasted sunflower seeds for garnish

Preheat the oven to 350°F (180°C).

Meanwhile bring the water and salt to a rolling boil in a medium pot. Stir in the wheat berries and return to a boil. Reduce the heat to medium and cook until the kernels are tender but chewy, about 1 hour. Remove from the heat and cool to room temperature in the liquid. Drain and set aside until needed.

Place the squash in a roasting pan. Add the garlic, drizzle with oil and toss well to evenly coat the squash. Season well with salt and pepper. Roast until the squash is soft and starting to brown, about 30 minutes. Remove from the oven and cool to room temperature.

Place the vinegar, garlic, sunflower seeds, apple juice and maple syrup in a blender and process until smooth. Thin with a little water, if necessary, to make a pouring consistency. Season with salt and pepper.

Place the wheat berries and squash in a large salad bowl. Add the dressing and toss well to coat. Garnish with the additional sunflower seeds and serve at room temperature.

Barley and Mushrooms with Pancetta Dressing

6 cups / 1.5 L water

1 tsp. / 5 mL salt

2 cups / 500 mL pearl barley

2 cups / 500 mL diced mushrooms

....

2 oz. / 60 g diced pancetta

1 tsp. / 5 mL minced garlic

1 medium onion, peeled and diced

2 Tbsp. / 30 mL chopped fresh Italian parsley

1 Tbsp. / 15 mL balsamic vinegar

1 Tbsp. / 15 mL olive oil

salt and black pepper to taste

....

1 medium tomato, seeded and chopped

2 Tbsp. / 30 mL grated Parmesan cheese

1 Tbsp. / 15 mL chopped fresh Italian parsley

PANCETTA

Italian-style, salt-cured, unsmoked bacon is called pancetta. It is rolled into a log and resembles salami. The meat is fatty and should be thinly sliced before cooking. Look for pancetta in Italian markets and some grocery stores. It is available in plain and spicy versions. Substitute any thinly sliced bacon.

Bring the water and salt to a rolling boil in a medium pot. Stir in the barley and bring back to a boil. Reduce the heat to medium and cook until the barley is just a little firm to the bite, about 35 minutes. Add the mushrooms and cook until the barley is tender, about 5 minutes. Drain and cool to room temperature.

Sauté the pancetta in a nonstick skillet over medium-high heat until just starting to crisp. Add the garlic and onion and sauté until the onion is soft and beginning to brown, about 2–3 minutes. Transfer to a salad bowl.

Add the 2 Tbsp. / 30 mL parsley, vinegar and oil to the salad bowl. Stir well and add the barley mixture. Toss well to mix, season with salt and pepper and garnish with the tomato, Parmesan cheese and remaining 1 Tbsp. / 5 mL parsley. Serve at room temperature.

Chilled Seafood Salads

Prawns and Mesclun with Tomato-Horseradish Dressing

4 cups / 1 L water

1 tsp. / 5 mL salt

1 tsp. / 5 mL sugar

1 lb. / 450 g large prawns (16–20 count), heads off

. . . .

1 lemon, juice and zest

1 tsp. / 5 mL minced garlic

1 Tbsp. / 15 mL grated horseradish

2 Tbsp. / 30 mL ketchup

2 Tbsp. / 30 mL olive oil

salt and black pepper to taste

. . . .

1 lb. / 450 g mesclun (or salad mix)

1 tomato, seeded and chopped

Place the water, salt and sugar in a medium pot. Bring to a boil, add the prawns and remove from the heat. Rest for 5 minutes. Drain the prawns and cool to handling temperature. Gently remove the shells and chill until needed.

Place the lemon juice, zest, garlic, horseradish, ketchup and olive oil in a mixing bowl. Whisk until smooth and season with salt and pepper. Add the mesclun to the dressing and toss well to coat. Garnish with the prawns and chopped tomato and serve immediately.

PRAWNS VS. SHRIMP

The terms *prawn* and *shrimp* are used almost interchangeably in many kitchens. In Europe, the term *prawn* is most often used for all sizes and species. In much of North America, *prawn* often refers to the larger sizes (raw or cooked) of shrimp and *shrimp* to the small, precooked varieties. These conventions are not always followed in stores and on restaurant menus. Prawns are often sold by count; this refers to the number of prawns per pound (such as 16–20 or 31–40). The larger the number, the smaller the prawn.

There are many prawn types available in our stores. Cultivated tiger prawns and white prawns are farmed in tropical climates (like Thailand and China) and shipped here frozen. Rock shrimp are harvested from the cold waters of eastern Canada to the warm waters of the Gulf of Mexico. The vast majority of commercial shrimp harvested are small pink shrimp and white or brown shrimp. These shrimp are generally sold cooked and shelled. The major west coast prawns are spot prawns, coonstripe prawns and sidestripe prawns.

Scallops and Shiitake Mushrooms with Balsamic Syrup

$1/4$ cup / 60 mL **balsamic vinegar**

1 Tbsp. / 15 mL **brown sugar**

1 tsp. / 5 mL **sesame oil**

1 tsp. / 5 mL **hot sauce (or to taste)**

1 tsp / 5 mL **cornstarch**

1 Tbsp. / 15 mL **water**

. . . .

1 Tbsp / 15 mL **minced garlic**

1 Tbsp. / 15 mL **chopped fresh chives**

1 large **egg**, beaten well

$1/4$ cup / 60 mL **cornstarch**

salt and black pepper to taste

$1/2$ lb. / 225 g **large sea scallops (cut in half, crosswise)**

1 lb. / 450 g **large whole shiitake mushrooms, stems removed**

2–6 Tbsp. / 30–90 mL **light oil**

. . . .

2 cups / 500 mL **shredded lettuce**

1 Tbsp. / 15 mL **toasted sesame seeds**

additional chives for garnish

To make the balsamic syrup, place the vinegar, sugar, sesame oil and hot sauce in a small pot and bring to a boil. Cook over high heat for 3–4 minutes, until the mixture is slightly reduced. Mix the 1 tsp. / 5 mL cornstarch with the water. Add it to the pot, stirring vigorously until the mixture thickens. Remove from the heat and cool to room temperature.

Combine the garlic, chives and egg in a medium bowl. Add the remaining $1/4$ cup / 60 mL cornstarch and mix into a thick batter. Season well with salt and pepper. Add the scallops and mushrooms and stir to coat.

Place 2 Tbsp. / 30 mL of the light oil in a large, nonstick pan over medium-high heat. Evenly cover the bottom of the pan with scallops and mushrooms (you may need to do this in two or three batches). Cook the pieces until they are golden brown, about 2–3 minutes per side. Transfer to a plate and repeat with the remaining slices, adding more oil each time. Cool to room temperature.

To serve, mound the shredded lettuce in the center of a serving platter. Top with the scallops and mushrooms. Drizzle with the balsamic syrup and garnish with sesame seeds and chives. Serve at room temperature.

Candied Salmon and Romaine with Clove-Mustard Vinaigrette

1 tsp. / 5 mL minced garlic

pinch ground cloves (or to taste)

1 Tbsp. / 15 mL sherry vinegar

1 Tbsp. / 15 mL grainy mustard

1 tsp. / 5 mL maple syrup

1 Tbsp. / 15 mL water

1/4 cup / 60 mL olive oil

salt and black pepper to taste

. . . .

1 head romaine lettuce

1/4 cup / 60 mL candied salmon, broken in chunks

1 recipe Garlic Croutons (page 51)

Place the garlic, cloves, vinegar, mustard, maple syrup and water in a mixing bowl. Drizzle in the oil, whisking constantly, until smooth and thick. Season with salt and pepper and set aside until needed.

Rinse the lettuce; rip the leaves into bite-size chunks and dry. Chill until needed.

Place the lettuce and candied salmon in a salad bowl, coat lightly with the dressing and toss well. Garnish with the croutons and serve immediately.

Smoked Sockeye Salmon and Tomatoes with Citrus Dressing

SERVES 4

1 lemon, juice and zest

1 lime, juice and zest

1 Tbsp. / 15 mL orange marmalade

$1/4$ cup / 60 mL mayonnaise

1 Tbsp. / 15 mL water

salt and black pepper to taste

. . . .

$1/4$ lb. / 115 g smoked sockeye salmon, thinly sliced

1 lb. / 450 g tomatoes

salt and black pepper to taste

1 green onion, thinly sliced

Place the lemon juice and zest, lime juice and zest, orange marmalade, mayonnaise and water in a mixing bowl. Whisk to mix and season with salt and pepper.

Arrange the salmon slices around the outside edge of a large platter. Cut the tomatoes into bite-size wedges (leave small tomatoes whole) and mound in the center of the platter. Season with salt and pepper. Drizzle the citrus dressing over top of the tomatoes and garnish with the green onion. Serve immediately.

Smoked Sablefish with Mustard Greens and Tomato-Basil Vinaigrette

1 cup / 250 mL **milk**

1/2 lb. / 225 g **smoked sablefish, cut in chunks**

. . . .

1 tsp. / 5 mL **minced garlic**

1 Tbsp. / 15 mL **red wine vinegar**

1 Tbsp. / 15 mL **water**

2 Tbsp. / 30 mL **chopped fresh basil**

1 medium **tomato, seeded and chopped**

2 Tbsp. / 30 mL **olive oil**

salt and black pepper to taste

. . . .

1 lb. / 450 g **mustard greens**

1 medium **tomato, seeded and chopped**

whole fresh basil leaves for garnish

Bring the milk to a boil in a small pot. Immediately remove from the heat, add the fish and let rest for 15 minutes. Drain the fish and cool to room temperature. The fish should flake easily at this point.

Place the garlic, vinegar, water, chopped basil, tomato and oil in a blender. Process until smooth and season with salt (lightly) and pepper. Strain the purée through a fine sieve into a salad bowl.

Add the fish and mustard greens to the dressing and toss well to coat. Garnish with the tomato and basil. Serve immediately.

VARIATIONS

Substitute smoked haddock or hot-smoked salmon for the sablefish. Use spinach or mixed greens in place of the mustard greens.

Hot-Smoked Salmon and Vegetables with Honey-Chili Vinaigrette

SERVES 4

1 tsp. / 5 mL minced garlic

1 tsp. / 5 mL minced ginger

1 lime, zest and juice

1 Tbsp. / 15 mL honey

1 tsp. / 5 mL chili paste (or to taste)

2 Tbsp. / 30 mL light oil

salt and black pepper to taste

· ·

1/2 lb. / 225 g hot-smoked salmon

2 cups / 500 mL sprouts (bean or sunflower)

2 cups / 500 mL shredded green cabbage

1 red bell pepper, thinly sliced

salt and black pepper to taste

additional sprouts for garnish

1 Tbsp. / 15 mL toasted sesame seeds

Place the garlic, ginger, lime juice, zest, honey and chili paste in a salad bowl. Drizzle in the oil, whisking constantly until smooth and thick. Season with salt and pepper and set aside until needed.

Add the smoked salmon, sprouts, cabbage and red pepper to the dressing. Season with salt and pepper and toss well to mix. Garnish with a small pile of sprouts and the sesame seeds. Serve immediately.

Barbecued Eel and Spinach with Soy-Sesame Dressing

1 Tbsp. / 15 mL rice vinegar

1 Tbsp. / 15 mL sweet soy sauce

1 Tbsp. / 15 mL minced pickled ginger

1 tsp. / 5 mL wasabi paste

1 Tbsp. / 15 mL water

1 tsp. / 5 mL sesame oil

2 Tbsp. / 30 mL light oil

salt and black pepper to taste

. . . .

1 lb. / 455 g baby spinach

$^1/_4$ lb. / 115 g barbecued eel, chopped on the diagonal

1 Tbsp. / 15 mL toasted sesame seeds

1 green onion, thinly sliced

Place the vinegar, soy sauce, pickled ginger, wasabi, water and sesame oil in a salad bowl. Drizzle in the light oil, whisking constantly, until smooth and thick. Season with salt and pepper and set aside until needed.

Add the spinach to the dressing and toss well to coat. Place the eel over the spinach. Garnish with the sesame seeds and green onion. Serve immediately.

BARBECUED EEL

Eel is a popular food in Asian cultures. In North America we most often see eel in Japanese restaurants and food stores. The two common types are *unagi* (freshwater eel) and *anago* (saltwater eel); both are truly delicious. Typically they are sold precooked — barbecued with a sweet soy glaze. You can substitute smoked salmon, sablefish or haddock.

Sea Urchin and Japanese Greens with Miso Dressing

1 tsp. / 5 mL minced garlic

1 lemon, juice only

1 Tbsp. / 15 mL light miso

1 Tbsp. / 15 mL mayonnaise

1 Tbsp. / 15 mL water

salt and black pepper to taste

. . . .

1 lb. / 450 g Japanese greens, such as mitsuba or mizuna

2 oz. / 60 g fresh sea urchin roe

1 Tbsp. / 15 mL chopped fresh chives

Place the garlic, lemon juice, miso, mayonnaise and water in a salad bowl. Whisk until smooth and season lightly with salt and pepper.

Add the Japanese greens and toss well to coat. Top the greens with the sea urchin and garnish with the chives. Serve immediately.

VARIATIONS

Substitute crabmeat for the sea urchin roe. Use spinach or mixed greens in place of the Japanese greens.

SEA URCHIN

The roe of sea urchin is a major delicacy in Japan, where it is called *uni*. The waters of the Pacific Northwest contain significant numbers of sea urchins and millions of pounds are harvested annually. Sea urchin is most often available as processed roe in Japanese markets, where it is sold fresh (anama uni), frozen (reito uni) and salted (shio uni). Occasionally, live whole urchins are available in Asian seafood markets. Red sea urchin is the most sought after, but purple and green varieties are also harvested. Fresh sea urchin has the finest flavor. Whole, unblemished roe is the most expensive and broken roe is considered secondary quality. Fresh urchin is smooth and buttery, tasting of the ocean — a rich and amazing flavor.

Poached Oysters and Squid with Peach Salsa

1 cup / 250 mL white wine

1 lb. / 450 g baby squid, cleaned

12 shucked oysters (with their juice)

. . . .

1 tsp. / 5 mL hot sauce (or to taste)

1 lime, juice and zest

4 tomatoes, seeded and finely diced

1 red bell pepper, seeded and finely diced

1 red onion, finely diced

2 cups / 500 mL diced fresh peach

1 Tbsp. / 15 mL chopped cilantro

salt and black pepper to taste

additional sprigs of cilantro for garnish

Place the wine in a medium pot and bring to a boil. Add the squid and bring back to a boil. Remove the pot from the heat and add the oysters with their juice. Allow to rest for 3–4 minutes. Remove the seafood with a slotted spoon, transfer to a container and chill until needed.

Return the remaining liquid to high heat. Reduce until about 2 Tbsp. / 30 mL of liquid remains. Cool to room temperature.

Combine the reduced cooking liquid, hot sauce, lime juice, zest, tomatoes, red pepper, onion, peach and cilantro in a serving bowl. Toss well to mix. Add the reserved squid and oysters and toss well to mix. Lightly season with salt and pepper. Garnish with cilantro sprigs and serve chilled.

SQUID

Squid comes in a multitude of sizes and is widely available in fish market and large grocery stores. Baby squid is very tender and the small tentacles make a great presentation. Large, fleshy body tubes can also be purchased. Shred these into tiny strips before continuing with the recipe. Cuttlefish, a close cousin of squid, is a good (and economical) substitute. Squid has a firm texture and delicate flavor. Be careful not to overcook as it will toughen.

Halibut, Fennel and Garlic Ceviche

SERVES 4

1 tsp. / 5 mL minced garlic

1 lime, juice and zest

1 lemon, juice and zest

$^1/_2$ cup / 125 mL white wine

1 Tbsp. / 15 mL honey

1 tsp. / 5 mL minced jalapeño pepper (seeds removed)

1 Tbsp. / 15 mL chopped fresh cilantro

1 Tbsp. / 15 mL chopped fresh fennel leaves

salt and black pepper to taste

. . . .

1 lb. / 450 g fresh halibut, cut in thin slices

1 bulb fennel, cut in paper-thin slices

additional cilantro sprigs for garnish

Place the garlic, lime juice and zest, lemon juice and zest, white wine, honey, jalapeño, chopped cilantro and fennel leaves in a nonreactive (preferably glass) bowl. Stir well to mix and season with salt and pepper.

Add the sliced halibut and fennel, tossing gently to mix. Cover with plastic wrap and chill for at least 1 hour (to a maximum of 6 hours). Just before serving, toss gently and garnish with cilantro sprigs. Serve chilled or at room temperature.

CEVICHE

Ceviche is a traditional raw/marinated fish dish in Latin America. It is very important that only the freshest, highest quality fish be used. The raw fish is marinated in citrus juice, herbs and spices. The citric acid produces a mild pickling effect, inhibiting bacterial growth and "cooking" the flesh — removing the raw fish flavor and turning the flesh opaque.

Warm Salads

Tofu and Pea Tops in Black Bean Vinaigrette

SERVES 4

1 Tbsp. / 15 mL light oil
1 Tbsp. / 15 mL minced ginger
2 Tbsp. / 30 mL black bean paste
1 Tbsp. / 15 mL balsamic vinegar
1 tsp. / 5 mL sesame oil
1 tsp. / 5 mL hot sauce (or to taste)
1 Tbsp. / 15 mL chopped cilantro
1 Tbsp. / 15 mL water
. . . .
$1/2$ cup / 125 mL diced firm tofu
$1/2$ lb. / 225 g pea tops
2 cups / 500 mL sprouts (bean, sunflower, etc.)
1 green onion, thinly sliced
additional cilantro sprigs for garnish

Cook the oil and ginger in a large nonstick pan over medium-high heat until sizzling. Stir in the black bean paste, vinegar, sesame oil, hot sauce, chopped cilantro and water. Cook until the mixture bubbles.

Add the tofu and pea tops. Toss well to mix. Stir until the greens just begin to wilt, about 1 minute. Add the sprouts, remove from the heat and toss well to mix. Transfer to a serving platter and garnish with the green onion and cilantro. Serve immediately.

Asparagus and Avocado Sushi Rice Salad

1 cup / 250 mL **sushi rice**

2 cups / 500 mL **water**

1 tsp. / 5 mL **salt**

2 Tbsp. / 30 mL **rice vinegar**

1 Tbsp. / 15 mL **sugar**

1 Tbsp. / 15 mL **salt**

. . . .

1/4 cup / 60 mL **light soy sauce**

2 tsp. / 10 mL **wasabi paste**

1 **lemon, juice and zest**

3 Tbsp. / 45 mL **chopped pickled ginger**

1 Tbsp. / 15 mL **mayonnaise**

. . . .

1 Tbsp. / 15 mL **light oil**

1 lb. / 450 g **asparagus, trimmed and thinly sliced**

salt and black pepper to taste

2 **avocados, peeled and chopped**

1 sheet **sushi nori, chopped in small pieces (see page 52)**

1 Tbsp. / 15 mL **toasted sesame seeds**

In a medium pot with a tight-fitting lid, rinse the rice under cold water, rubbing to release the starch. Rinse until the water becomes clear. Drain the rice, add the 2 cups / 500 mL water and the 1 tsp. / 5 mL salt. Place over high heat and bring to a boil. Reduce the heat to low, cover and cook for 20 minutes. Remove the pot from the heat and let stand for 10 minutes.

Place the vinegar, sugar and 1 Tbsp. / 15 mL salt in a small bowl. Stir well to mix. Turn the rice out into a large baking sheet (or bowl) and sprinkle with the vinegar mixture. With a wooden utensil, stir the rice until it is well mixed and beginning to cool. Cover with a clean towel and keep warm until needed.

Place the soy sauce, wasabi, lemon juice and zest, pickled ginger and mayonnaise in a small bowl. Stir well to mix and set aside.

Heat the oil in a large wok or nonstick pan over high heat until almost smoking. Add the asparagus and season well with salt and pepper. Sauté until tender, about 3–4 minutes.

Add the asparagus and avocados to the dressing. Toss well to coat. Add the rice to the bowl and toss well to mix. Garnish with the nori and sesame seeds and serve immediately.

Wok-seared Cabbage with Cranberry-Mustard Dressing

SERVES 4

1 Tbsp. / 15 mL white balsamic vinegar

2 Tbsp. / 30 mL chopped dried cranberries

1 Tbsp. / 15 mL grainy mustard

1 Tbsp. / 15 mL orange juice (or water)

3 Tbsp. / 45 mL olive oil

salt and black pepper to taste

. . . .

1 Tbsp. / 15 mL light oil

1 head shredded green cabbage

1 yellow bell pepper, seeded and thinly sliced

1 Tbsp. / 15 mL minced garlic

$1/4$ cup / 125 mL toasted sunflower seeds

Place the vinegar, cranberries, mustard and orange juice in a large salad bowl. Drizzle in the olive oil, whisking constantly, until smooth and thick. Season with salt and pepper and set aside until needed.

Heat the light oil in a large wok or nonstick pan over high heat until almost smoking. Add the cabbage and bell pepper and quickly stir-fry until the vegetables just begin to brown and become tender, about 4–5 minutes. Add the garlic and cook until fragrant, about 1 minute. Remove from the heat and add to the dressing. Toss well to coat. Garnish with the sunflower seeds and serve immediately.

Thai-Style Turkey with Spinach

$^{1}/_{2}$ lb. / 225 g turkey breast, cut in thin strips

$^{1}/_{4}$ cup / 60 mL cornstarch

salt and black pepper to taste

3 Tbsp. / 45 mL light oil

. . . .

$^{1}/_{2}$ cup / 125 mL coconut milk

1 Tbsp. / 15 mL minced ginger

1 Tbsp. / 15 mL minced garlic

1 Tbsp. / 15 mL curry paste (or to taste)

1 Tbsp. / 15 mL fish sauce (see page 90)

1 lime, juice and zest

. . . .

1 lb. / 450 g spinach, washed and dried

2 Tbsp. / 30 mL chopped dry roasted peanuts

1 Tbsp. / 15 mL chopped fresh basil

Place the turkey breast and cornstarch in a mixing bowl. Toss to coat and season well with salt and pepper.

Heat the oil in a large wok, or nonstick pan over high heat until almost smoking. Add the turkey and toss well to break up the pieces. Sauté until the turkey is cooked through but still moist, about 4–5 minutes. Remove from the heat and transfer to a platter covered in paper towels to absorb excess oil. Keep warm until needed.

Remove all fat from the pan and add the coconut milk, ginger, garlic, curry paste, fish sauce, lime juice and zest. Bring to a boil over medium-high heat, reduce to a simmer and cook for 5 minutes.

Place the spinach in a salad bowl. Add the turkey to the sauce and heat through. Combine the turkey mixture with the spinach and toss well to coat. Garnish with the peanuts and basil and serve immediately.

Maple-Glazed Duck Breast over Greens and Wild Mushrooms

2 Tbsp. / 30 mL **maple syrup**

2 Tbsp. / 30 mL **balsamic vinegar**

1 tsp. / 5 mL **minced garlic**

1 Tbsp. / 15 mL **soy sauce**

1 tsp. / 5 mL **hot sauce**

. . . .

2 **duck breasts, trimmed of excess fat**

salt and black pepper to taste

. . . .

1 Tbsp. / 15 mL **olive oil**

1 tsp. / 5 mL **minced garlic**

1 tsp. / 5 mL **minced fresh rosemary**

2 cups / 500 mL **sliced wild mushrooms**

1 lb. / 450 g **greens (kale, spinach, mustard, etc.)**

Place the maple syrup, vinegar, 1 tsp. / 5 mL garlic, soy sauce and hot sauce in a nonreactive saucepan. Bring to a boil over high heat and cook until the volume is reduced by half. Set aside.

Prepare the duck by lightly cutting the skin with a sharp knife — cutting into the fat but not into the flesh. Season well with salt and pepper. Place the duck breasts in a nonstick pan over medium heat and cook, fat side down, for 8–9 minutes, or until golden brown. Flip the breasts and cook for an additional 2–3 minutes, or until lightly browned. Brush with a little of the glaze and allow to brown slightly, about 1 minute per side. Transfer to a plate and rest for at least 5 minutes. Keep warm until needed.

Remove the fat from the pan. Add the remaining olive oil, remaining 1 tsp. / 5 mL garlic and rosemary and heat until sizzling. Add the mushrooms and sauté until cooked through, about 5–7 minutes. The mushrooms will release their juices into the pan; continue cooking until all the moisture has evaporated. Add the greens and toss to wilt slightly.

Place the mixture on a serving plate. Slice the duck breast thinly and place it on top, along with any juice released. Drizzle with the remaining glaze. Serve immediately.

MUSHROOMS

Many types of wild mushrooms are available in our markets. Chanterelles and porcini are the most common. Morels are often available in the spring. Cultivated mushrooms such as oyster, shiitake and button (including white button, brown button, portobello) are all excellent substitutes. To prepare wild mushrooms, cut off any discolored edges, brush off any debris and slice. If they are really dirty, brush them with a clean, damp kitchen towel.

Grilled Pancetta-Wrapped Radicchio with Balsamic Dressing

1 medium **tomato**, seeded and chopped

1 Tbsp. / 15 mL **chopped fresh basil**

$^1/_2$ cup / 125 mL **diced mozzarella cheese**

salt and black pepper to taste

· ·

1 head **radicchio**

4 thin slices **pancetta**

2 Tbsp. / 30 mL **olive oil**, divided

salt and black pepper to taste

1 Tbsp. / 15 mL **balsamic vinegar**

1 medium **tomato**, seeded and diced

Preheat the grill to high.

Combine the tomato, basil and mozzarella cheese in a small bowl. Season with salt and pepper and mix well.

Break the radicchio into individual leaves. Fill 4 large leaves with a little of the tomato mixture and roll each up in a cigar shape. Lay out a strip of pancetta and place the radicchio roll on one end. Roll it up, wrapping the pancetta in a tight strip around the middle of the roll. Secure with a wooden toothpick or short skewer. Repeat with the remaining 3 leaves. Drizzle lightly with 1 Tbsp./15 mL of the olive oil and season well with salt and pepper. Set aside until needed.

Grill the rolls until the pancetta begins to brown and the radicchio has wilted and is slightly charred. Transfer to a serving plate and drizzle with the remaining 1 Tbsp. / 15 mL of olive oil and the balsamic vinegar. Garnish with the diced tomato and serve warm.

Mustard Greens and Tomatoes with Warm Bacon Dressing

4 slices **smoked bacon, minced**

1 medium **onion, diced**

$^1/_2$ cup / 125 mL **diced mushrooms**

2 Tbsp. / 30 mL **balsamic vinegar**

2 Tbsp. / 30 mL **olive oil**

. . . .

1 lb. / 450 g **mustard greens**

2 medium **tomatoes, seeded and chopped**

1 Tbsp. / 15 mL **chopped fresh Italian parsley**

1 Tbsp. / 15 mL **grated Parmesan cheese**

Sauté the bacon in a large, nonstick pan over medium-high heat. Add the onion and mushrooms and cook until soft and just beginning to brown, about 5 minutes. Remove the excess fat with a spoon (or soak it up with a paper towel). Stir in the vinegar and oil.

Place the mustard greens and tomatoes in a salad bowl, top with the warm bacon dressing and toss well to coat. Garnish with parsley and Parmesan cheese and serve immediately.

Kale with Onion Marmalade and Ham

SERVES 4

1 Tbsp. / 15 mL light oil
1 Tbsp. / 15 mL minced garlic
2 medium onions, sliced
2 Tbsp. / 30 mL marmalade
1 Tbsp. / 15 mL sherry vinegar
$^1/_4$ cup / 60 mL white wine
salt and black pepper to taste
. . . .
1 Tbsp. / 15 mL olive oil
1 tsp. / 5 mL minced ginger
1 lb. / 450 g shredded kale
2 Tbsp. / 30 mL water
$^1/_2$ cup / 125 mL shredded smoked ham
1 Tbsp. / 15 mL minced green olives

Sauté the light oil and garlic in a large, nonstick pan over medium-high heat until sizzling. Add the onions and toss well. Sauté until the onions soften and begin to brown, about 5 minutes. Add the marmalade and sauté until the onions begin to darken deeply in color, about 2 minutes. Add the vinegar and wine and cook until all the liquid has evaporated. Season with salt and pepper. Transfer to a bowl and set aside until needed.

Return the pan to the heat, add the olive oil, ginger, kale and water. Cook, stirring occasionally, until the kale has wilted and is tender, about 5 minutes. When most of the liquid has evaporated, add the onion mixture and toss well to coat. Transfer to a serving platter and top with the ham and olives. Serve immediately.

Crab and Spinach Salad with Soy-Onion Aïoli

SERVES 4

$^1/_4$ cup / 60 mL **mayonnaise**

1 Tbsp. / 15 mL **sweet soy sauce**

1 tsp. / 5 mL **minced garlic**

1 tsp. / 5 mL **chili sauce (or hot sauce to taste)**

1 **green onion, minced**

. . . .

1 Tbsp. / 15 mL **light oil**

1 Tbsp. / 15 mL **minced garlic**

1 lb. / 450 g **spinach**

$^1/_4$ lb. / 115 g **cooked crabmeat**

1 Tbsp. / 15 mL **toasted sesame seeds**

To make the aïoli, combine the mayonnaise, sweet soy sauce, garlic, chili sauce and green onion in a mixing bowl. Whisk until smooth and set aside.

Sauté the oil and garlic in a large nonstick pan over medium-high heat until sizzling. Add the spinach and toss until the leaves just wilt, about 1 minute. Add the crabmeat and sauté until heated through, about 1 minute.

Mound the salad on a serving platter. Drizzle the soy-onion aïoli on top and around the greens. Garnish with sesame seeds and serve immediately.

Crusted Oysters with Sweet Chili Dressing over Coleslaw

1 tsp. / 5 mL chili paste (or hot sauce to taste)

2 Tbsp. / 30 mL honey

1 lemon, juice and zest

1 Tbsp. / 15 mL mayonnaise (or sour cream)

. . . .

1 cup / 250 mL cornmeal

2 Tbsp. / 30 mL grated Parmesan cheese

3 Tbsp. / 45 mL chopped toasted pumpkin seeds

1 Tbsp / 15 mL chopped fresh parsley

salt and black pepper to taste

. . . .

2 Tbsp. / 30 mL olive oil

12 large oysters, shucked

1 recipe Coleslaw with a Grainy Mustard and Herb Dressing
   (page 76)

additional chopped fresh parsley for garnish

additional toasted pumpkin seeds for garnish

To make the sweet chili dressing, combine the chili paste, honey, lemon juice, zest and mayonnaise in a small bowl. Whisk until smooth and set aside.

Combine the cornmeal, cheese, 3 Tbsp. / 45 mL pumpkin seeds and 1 Tbsp. / 15 mL parsley on a plate. Season well with salt and pepper and stir well to mix.

Heat the oil in a large nonstick pan over medium-high heat until very hot. Cook the oysters (in batches of 6) until crispy and golden, about 3–4 minutes per side. Transfer the cooked oysters to a plate lined with paper towel and keep warm.

Use a slotted spoon to transfer the coleslaw to a serving platter, leaving the liquid behind. Place the oysters on top and drizzle with the sweet chili dressing. Garnish with parsley and pumpkin seeds and serve immediately.

Potato & Root Salads

Curried Potato and Yam

SERVES 4

1 lb. / 450 g peeled and diced potatoes

2 cups / 500 mL peeled and diced yam

1 Tbsp. / 15 mL salt

1 medium onion, diced

. . . .

¹/₄ cup / 60 mL mayonnaise

1 tsp. / 5 mL curry paste

1 Tbsp. / 15 mL minced ginger

1 Tbsp. / 15 mL chopped cilantro

1 lime, juice and zest

salt and black pepper to taste

. . . .

2 Tbsp. / 30 mL chopped peanuts

1 green onion, thinly sliced

lime wedges for garnish

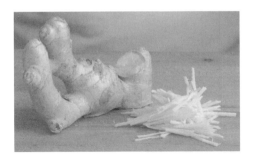

Place the potatoes and yam in a large pot, cover generously with cold water and add the salt. Bring to a boil over high heat, then reduce the heat to medium-high. Cook until the vegetables are tender, about 10 minutes. Add the diced onion and cook for 1 minute. Drain and set aside to cool to room temperature.

Combine the mayonnaise, curry paste, ginger, cilantro, lime juice and zest in a salad bowl. Add the cooked vegetables, season with salt and pepper and gently toss to coat. Garnish with the peanuts, green onion and lime wedges. Serve at room temperature.

Potato and Sauerkraut with Ham and Apples

2 lbs. / 900 g small new potatoes, washed and halved

1 Tbsp. / 15 mL salt

1 cup / 250 mL sauerkraut

. . . .

2 Tbsp. / 30 mL apple cider vinegar

$^{1}/_{4}$ cup / 60 mL olive oil

salt and black pepper to taste

$^{1}/_{2}$ cup / 125 mL diced ham

2 apples, peeled, cored and diced

2 Tbsp. / 30 mL chopped fresh parsley

Place the potatoes in a large pot, cover generously with cold water and add the salt. Bring to a boil over high heat, then reduce the heat to medium-high. Cook until the potatoes are tender, about 8–10 minutes. Add the sauerkraut and bring back to a boil. Remove from the heat and drain.

Place the hot potato mixture in a large salad bowl and drizzle with the vinegar and oil. Toss well to mix and season with salt and pepper. Add the ham, apples and parsley and toss well to mix. Serve at room temperature.

Purple Potatoes with Pesto Sour Cream

2 lbs. / 900 g new purple potatoes, washed

1 Tbsp. / 15 mL salt

. . . .

1/4 cup / 60 mL chopped fresh basil

1 Tbsp. / 15 mL minced garlic

1 Tbsp. / 15 mL grated Parmesan cheese

2 Tbsp. / 30 mL olive oil

1/4 cup / 60 mL sour cream

salt and black pepper to taste

additional basil leaves for garnish

Place the potatoes in a large pot, cover generously with cold water and add the salt. Bring to a boil over high heat, then reduce the heat to medium-high. Cook until the potatoes are tender, about 8–10 minutes. Drain and set aside.

Place the chopped basil, garlic, Parmesan cheese, olive oil and sour cream in a blender. Process until smooth and season with salt and pepper.

Cut the potatoes into thin slices and place in a salad bowl. Add the dressing and toss well to mix. Serve immediately or store in the refrigerator until needed. Just before serving, garnish with additional basil leaves

POTATOES

The humble potato has been part of our diet for millennia (dating back over 11,000 years in the Andes of Peru). Wild plants are found throughout Central and South America. The potato is now grown around the globe and is the world's fourth-largest food crop. There are literally hundreds of varieties and modern cultivars continue to be developed. Many exotic and beautiful varieties are available, such as Peruvian purple potatoes, Russian fingerlings, pink fir apple, Yukon gold and many others. All green parts of the plant, including tubers exposed to light, contain a toxin (solanine), which has been linked to gastrointestinal disturbances and neurological disorders. It is important to remove any green peel before cooking.

Yukon Gold Potato and Bacon Salad

SERVES 4–6

2 lbs. / 900 g Yukon gold potatoes, peeled and thickly sliced

1 Tbsp. / 15 mL salt

. . . .

4 slices smoked bacon, chopped

1 medium onion, thinly sliced

1 Tbsp. / 15 mL minced garlic

1 Tbsp. / 15 mL grainy mustard

2 Tbsp. / 30 mL white wine vinegar

salt and black pepper to taste

1 Tbsp. / 15 mL chopped fresh parsley

Place the potatoes in a large pot, cover generously with cold water and add the salt. Bring to a boil over high heat, then reduce the heat to medium-high. Cook until the potatoes are tender, about 8–10 minutes. Drain and set aside.

Cook the bacon in a nonstick pan over medium-high heat until it is beginning to crisp, about 5 minutes. Add the onion and cook until soft, about 2–3 minutes. Remove the excess fat with a spoon (or blot it up with a paper towel). Stir in the mustard and vinegar and remove from the heat.

Pour the dressing over the potatoes while still warm and toss gently to mix. Season well with salt and pepper. Garnish with parsley and serve warm or at room temperature.

Potato Salad with Pickled Beet Dressing

SERVES 4–6

2 lbs. / 900 g new red-skinned potatoes, washed and quartered

1 Tbsp. / 15 mL salt

. . . .

$^1/_2$ cup / 125 mL sour cream

$^1/_2$ cup / 125 mL coarsely chopped pickled beets

4 large eggs, hard-boiled and peeled

salt and black pepper to taste

1 Tbsp. / 15 mL chopped fresh chives

Place the potatoes in a large pot, cover generously with cold water and add the salt. Bring to a boil over high heat, then reduce the heat to medium-high. Cook until the potatoes are tender, about 8–10 minutes. Drain and set aside.

Combine the sour cream and pickled beets in a salad bowl. Stir well to mix. Slice the eggs and add to the dressing along with the potatoes. Season with salt and pepper. Toss well to coat. Garnish with the chives and serve immediately.

Grated Celariac with Creamy Poppy Seed Dressing

1 cup / 250 mL yogurt

1 lemon, juice and zest

1 Tbsp. / 15 mL honey

1 Tbsp. / 15 mL poppy seeds

salt and black pepper to taste

. . . .

4 cups / 1 L shredded celeriac

additional poppy seeds for garnish

Combine the yogurt, lemon juice, zest, honey and poppy seeds in a large salad bowl. Season well with salt and pepper.

Add the celeriac and toss to coat. Rest for at least 10 minutes. Before serving, stir well and adjust the seasoning with salt and pepper. Garnish with poppy seeds.

CELERIAC

Sometimes called celery root, celeriac is a close cousin of the common celery plant. Unlike celery, it is the swollen base and root of the vegetable that is eaten (the leaves are very bitter). The flavor is distinctly celery-like and it can be eaten raw or cooked. It is a great, seldom-used vegetable that makes an intriguing addition to stews and is wonderful as a purée. The exterior is rough and gnarled and often contains pockets of dirt and sand. Rinse well before preparing and carefully cut away the rough outer layer, until the mottled-white flesh is exposed. Shred using a cheese grater, food processor or julienne slicer.

Maple-Roasted Onion Salad with Apple-Walnut Dressing

4 large white onions, thickly sliced

2 Tbsp. / 30 mL olive oil

salt and black pepper to taste

$^1/_2$ cup / 125 mL walnut halves

1 Tbsp. / 15 mL maple syrup

. . . .

1 Tbsp. / 15 mL apple cider vinegar

1 Tbsp. / 15 mL mustard

1 Tbsp. / 15 mL apple juice (or water)

1 apple, cored and finely diced

3 Tbsp. / 45 mL walnut oil (or olive oil)

salt and black pepper to taste

Preheat the oven to 375°F (190°C).

Spread the onion slices on a baking tray and drizzle with 1 Tbsp / 15 mL of the olive oil. Season with salt and pepper and flip the pieces. Drizzle the remaining 1 Tbsp. / 15 mL oil over top and season with salt and pepper. Place the tray in the oven and roast until the onions are soft and begin to brown, about 15 minutes. Scatter the walnuts on top and drizzle with the maple syrup. Return to the oven and cook until the walnuts begin to brown, about 5 minutes (do not let the walnuts burn). Remove from the oven and allow to cool to room temperature.

Place the vinegar, mustard, apple juice and apple in a salad bowl. Drizzle in the walnut oil, whisking constantly, until smooth and thick. Season with salt and pepper. Set aside until needed.

Scrape the cooled onions and walnuts into the bowl and toss well to mix. Serve at room temperature.

ROASTING VEGETABLES

Roasting is a great way to cook a variety of vegetables. It caramelizes the natural sugars, develops rich flavor and limits the nutrient loss. Use a heavy roasting pan for the best results. It's a good idea, particularly if you use aluminum trays, to line them with baking parchment. The food will not brown as easily on the bottom, so it's important to toss the vegetables halfway through cooking to ensure even browning. Oil also helps to promote even browning. If you are using sugar, honey or maple syrup, add it during the last 5–10 minutes of cooking. Make sure the sugars do not burn and transfer bitter flavors to the vegetables.

Roasted Beet Salad with Pickled Ginger Vinaigrette

4 medium beets, washed and trimmed

1 Tbsp. / 15 mL olive oil

salt and black pepper to taste

. . . .

3 Tbsp. / 45 mL rice vinegar

1 Tbsp. / 15 mL mustard

1 Tbsp. / 15 mL light soy sauce

2 Tbsp. / 30 mL chopped pickled ginger

1 Tbsp. / 15 mL brown sugar

3 Tbsp. / 45 mL light oil

salt and black pepper to taste

Preheat the oven to 375°F (190°C).

Place the beets in a roasting pan and drizzle with the olive oil. Season well with salt and pepper. Place in a hot oven and roast until a knife slides easily into the beets, at least 1 hour. Remove from the oven and cool.

Peel the beets and cut into thick slices. Cut each slice into cubes. Set aside until needed.

Place the vinegar, mustard, soy sauce, pickled ginger and brown sugar in a mixing bowl. Drizzle in the light oil, whisking constantly, until smooth and thick. Add the beets and toss well to coat. Season well with salt and lots of pepper and allow to sit for at least 10 minutes. Serve chilled or at room temperature.

BEETS

Beetroot evolved from the wild sea-beet of Western Asia and Europe. Beets come in a multitude of colors. Red, white, yellow, orange and multicolored versions are available. The common variety is blood red from the presence of betatin (widely used as a food colorant). It can easily stain hands, clothing and cutting boards. Wear disposable latex gloves and cover the cutting board with a sheet of plastic wrap if you want to minimize the damage. Beet tops are delicious salad greens when young, and make a hearty cooking green.

Baby Carrots with Mustard-Lime Dressing

SERVES 4–6

8 cups / 2 L water
1 Tbsp. / 15 mL salt
2 lbs. / 900 g baby carrots, washed and trimmed

· ·

2 Tbsp. / 30 mL mayonnaise
2 Tbsp. / 30 mL mustard
1 lime, juice and zest
1 tsp. / 5 mL honey
1 tsp. / 5 mL minced garlic
1 Tbsp. / 15 mL minced fresh sage
salt and black pepper to taste
2 Tbsp. / 30 mL toasted sunflower seeds

Bring the water and salt to a boil in a large pot. Add the carrots and cook until just tender, about 6–7 minutes. Drain in a colander and rinse with cold water to cool. Chill until needed.

Combine the mayonnaise, mustard, lime juice, zest, honey, garlic and sage in a salad bowl. Whisk until smooth.

Add the chilled carrots to the dressing and toss well to coat. Season well with salt and pepper. Garnish with the sunflower seeds and serve immediately.

Shredded Carrot and Daikon with Mirin Vinaigrette

2 Tbsp. / 30 mL mirin (sweetened rice wine)

1 Tbsp. / 15 mL miso

1 lemon, juice and zest

1 tsp. / 5 mL honey

1 tsp. / 5 mL minced garlic

1 tsp. / 5 mL minced ginger

2 Tbsp / 30 mL light oil

salt and black pepper to taste

. . . .

2 cups / 500 mL shredded carrot

2 cups / 500 mL shredded daikon

2 Tbsp. / 30 mL toasted sesame seeds

Place the mirin, miso, lemon juice, zest, honey, garlic and ginger in a mixing bowl. Drizzle in the oil, whisking constantly, until smooth and thick. Season lightly with salt and pepper.

Add the carrot and daikon to the dressing and toss well to mix. Just before serving, garnish with the sesame seeds.

DAIKON

Most often known by the Japanese name of daikon, white radish is delicious raw or cooked. It is rich in vitamin C, iron and calcium and contains the enzyme diatase (excellent for calming the stomach). The roots can be huge, many over 12 inches (30 cm) in length. Lightly peel or scrub them before use. Daikon is an excellent addition to any salad and grated daikon makes a great condiment for Japanese dishes.

Hand-Held Salads

Tortilla Roll with Mixed Greens, Tomatoes and Olives

1 Tbsp. / 15 mL red wine vinegar

1 Tbsp. / 15 mL chopped fresh basil

1 Tbsp. / 15 mL chopped fresh Italian parsley

1 tsp. / 5 mL minced garlic

2 Tbsp. / 30 mL olive oil

salt and black pepper to taste

2 medium tomatoes, seeded and chopped

¼ cup / 60 mL sliced mixed olives

2 cups / 500 mL mixed greens

1 Tbsp. / 15 mL shredded Parmesan cheese

4 large tortillas

Place the vinegar, basil, parsley and garlic in a mixing bowl. Drizzle in the oil, whisking constantly, until smooth and thick. Season with salt and pepper. Add the tomatoes, olives, mixed greens and Parmesan cheese to the dressing and toss to coat.

Lay a tortilla on a clean cutting board. Place about 1 cup / 250 mL of the salad along the edge closest to you, leaving any excess dressing behind. Fold the edge closest to you over the salad and squeeze gently to form a compact log of filling. Fold one end of the tortilla about 1 inch / 2.5 cm over the log. Continue to roll the tortilla into a compact cylinder.

Place the tortilla seam side down on a plate and repeat with the remaining ingredients. Serve immediately.

Tortilla Roll with Tuna Salad, Shredded Lettuce and Cheddar

SERVES 4

1 can (3 $^1/_2$ oz) / 100 g **tuna**, drained

2 Tbsp. / 30 mL **mayonnaise**

1 Tbsp. / 15 mL **sweet green relish**

1 **green onion**, minced

salt and black pepper to taste

. . . .

2 cups / 500 mL **shredded lettuce**

$^1/_2$ cup / 125 mL **grated Cheddar cheese**

4 large **tortillas**

Combine the tuna, mayonnaise, relish and green onion in a small mixing bowl. Stir well to mix and season with salt and pepper.

Lay a tortilla on a clean cutting board. Place about $^1/_2$ cup / 250 mL of the lettuce along the edge closest to you. Top with $^1/_4$ of the tuna mixture and $^1/_4$ of the cheese. Fold the edge closest to you over the salad and squeeze gently to form a compact log of filling. Fold one end of the tortilla about 1 inch / 2.5 cm over the log. Continue to roll the tortilla into a compact cylinder.

Place the tortilla seam side down on a plate and repeat with the remaining ingredients. Serve immediately.

Tortilla Roll with Barbecued Duck, Mesclun and Hoisin Aïoli

$^1/_4$ cup / 60 mL mayonnaise

1 Tbsp. / 15 mL hoisin sauce

1 tsp. / 5 mL minced garlic

1 tsp. / 5 mL sesame oil

1 tsp. / 5 mL hot sauce (or to taste)

. . . .

2 cups / 500 L mesclun

1 cup / 250 mL shredded Chinese barbecued duck
  (or cooked chicken)

1 cup / 250 mL diced seedless cucumber

1 Tbsp. / 15 mL toasted sesame seeds (see page 46)

4 large tortillas

Combine the mayonnaise, hoisin sauce, garlic, sesame oil and hot sauce in a mixing bowl. Stir well.

Lay a tortilla on a clean cutting board. Place about $^1/_2$ cup / 125 mL of the mesclun along the edge closest to you. Top with $^1/_4$ of the duck meat and $^1/_4$ of the cucumber. Evenly spread $^1/_4$ of the hoisin mixture on top of the filling. Fold the edge closest to you over the salad and squeeze gently to form a compact log of filling. Fold one end of the tortilla about 1 inch / 2.5 cm over the log. Continue to roll the tortilla into a compact cylinder.

Place the tortilla seam side down on a plate and repeat with the remaining ingredients. Serve immediately.

Tortilla Roll with Rice Noodles and Vegetables in Black Bean Dressing

1 Tbsp. / 15 mL black bean paste
1 Tbsp. / 15 mL rice vinegar
1 tsp. / 5 mL minced ginger
1 Tbsp. / 15 mL chopped cilantro
1 tsp. / 5 mL sesame oil
2 Tbsp. / 30 mL light oil
black pepper to taste
. . . .
1 cup / 250 mL chopped fresh (or dried) rice noodles
1 red bell pepper, cored and chopped
1 cup / 250 mL diced seedless cucumber
1 tomato, seeded and chopped
1 cup / 250 mL chopped spinach
4 large tortillas

Place the black bean paste, vinegar, ginger, cilantro and sesame oil in a mixing bowl. Drizzle in the light oil, whisking constantly, until smooth and thick. Season with pepper and set aside until needed.

Place the noodles in a heat-proof bowl and cover with boiling water. Swirl to mix. Drain the noodles when softened and plump, about 1 minute (or 10 minutes for dried).

Add the noodles, red pepper, cucumber, tomato and spinach to the dressing. Toss well to coat.

Lay a tortilla on a clean cutting board. Place about 1 cup / 250 mL of the noodle mixture along the edge closest to you, leaving any excess dressing behind. Fold the edge closest to you over the noodle mixture and squeeze gently to form a compact log of filling. Fold one end of the tortilla about 1 inch / 2.5 cm over the log. Continue to roll the tortilla into a compact cylinder.

Place the tortilla seam side down on a plate and repeat with the remaining ingredients. Serve immediately.

Pita Stuffed with Greek Salad in Herb Vinaigrette

1 Tbsp. / 15 mL white wine vinegar

1 Tbsp. / 15 mL chopped fresh marjoram

1 Tbsp. / 15 mL chopped fresh Italian parsley

1 tsp. / 5 mL minced garlic

2 Tbsp. / 30 mL olive oil

salt and black pepper to taste

. . . .

2 medium tomatoes, chopped

$^1/_4$ cup / 60 mL sliced mixed olives

1 cup / 250 mL diced seedless cucumber

$^1/_2$ cup / 125 mL crumbled feta cheese

2 cups / 500 mL chopped head lettuce

2 large pita breads

Place the vinegar, marjoram, parsley and garlic in a mixing bowl. Drizzle in the oil, whisking constantly, until smooth and thick. Season with salt and pepper.

Add the tomatoes, olives, cucumber, feta and lettuce to the dressing and toss to coat.

Cut the pitas in half. Open one half with your fingers to form a pocket. Fill with $^1/_4$ of the salad mixture and place in the middle of a folded napkin. Repeat with the remaining ingredients and serve immediately.

Pita Stuffed with Mushrooms, Spinach and Goat Cheese

SERVES 4

1 Tbsp. / 15 mL olive oil

1 Tbsp. / 15 mL minced garlic

1 cup / 250 mL sliced mushrooms (such as button,
  oyster or shiitake)

salt and black pepper to taste

. . . .

1 Tbsp. / 15 mL balsamic vinegar

1 Tbsp. / 15 mL chopped fresh thyme (or rosemary or marjoram)

1 tsp. / 5 mL minced garlic

2 Tbsp. / 30 mL olive oil

$^1/_2$ cup / 125 mL soft goat cheese

2 cups / 500 mL baby spinach

2 large pita breads

Heat the olive oil and garlic in a nonstick pan over medium-high heat until sizzling. Add the mushrooms, season with salt and pepper and sauté until soft and beginning to brown, about 4–5 minutes. Remove from the heat and cool.

Place the vinegar, thyme and garlic in a mixing bowl. Drizzle in the oil, whisking constantly, until smooth and thick. Break the goat cheese into small lumps and add to the dressing along with the spinach and mushrooms. Toss well to coat and season again with salt and pepper.

Cut the pitas in half. Open one half with your fingers to form a pocket. Fill with $^1/_4$ of the salad mixture and place in the middle of a folded napkin. Repeat with the remaining ingredients and serve immediately.

Pita Stuffed with Smoked Chicken, Romaine and Maple-Mustard Dressing

SERVES 4

1 lemon, juice and zest

1 Tbsp. / 15 mL maple syrup

2 Tbsp. / 30 mL mayonnaise

1 Tbsp. / 15 mL minced fresh sage

1 Tbsp. / 15 mL mustard

1 tsp. / 5 mL minced garlic

salt and black pepper

1 cup / 250 mL diced smoked chicken

4 cups / 1 L chopped head lettuce

2 large pita breads

2 Tbsp. / 30 mL Parmesan cheese

Combine the lemon juice, zest, maple syrup, mayonnaise, sage, mustard and garlic in a mixing bowl. Stir well to mix and season with salt and lots of pepper. Add the chicken and lettuce and toss well to coat.

Cut the pitas in half. Open one half with your fingers to form a pocket. Fill with 1/4 of the salad mixture, top with a sprinkle of Parmesan cheese and place in the middle of a folded napkin. Repeat with the remaining ingredients and serve immediately.

Pita Stuffed with Tomatoes, Bocconcini and Balsamic Dressing

1 Tbsp. / 15 mL balsamic vinegar

1 Tbsp. / 15 mL chopped fresh basil

1 tsp. / 5 mL minced garlic

2 Tbsp. / 30 mL olive oil

salt and black pepper to taste

2 medium tomatoes, chopped

4 small fresh bocconcini, sliced

2 cups / 500 mL chopped head lettuce

2 large pita breads

basil sprigs for garnish

Place the vinegar, chopped basil and garlic in a mixing bowl. Drizzle in the oil, whisking constantly, until smooth and thick. Season with salt and pepper. Add the tomatoes and bocconcini and toss well to coat. Allow to rest for at least 5 minutes. Add the lettuce and toss to coat.

Cut the pitas in half. Open one half with your fingers to form a pocket. Fill with ¼ of the salad mixture, garnish with a sprig of basil and place in the middle of a folded napkin. Repeat with the remaining ingredients and serve immediately.

BOCCONCINI

Small balls of fresh mozzarella are sold as bocconcini. The majority of the cheeses are made from cow's milk, but the finest (and most expensive) cheeses are made from buffalo milk. The cheese is soft, creamy and excellent fresh, particularly when paired with tomatoes. Bocconcini are sold in containers filled with salted water. The cheese is fairly perishable and should be used up within 2–3 days of purchase. Its soft texture readily absorbs marinades.

Rice Paper Rolls with Salami, Provolone, Red Onion and Arugula

SERVES 4

1 Tbsp. / 15 mL red wine vinegar

1 Tbsp. / 15 mL chopped fresh basil

1 Tbsp. / 15 mL chopped fresh marjoram

1 tsp. / 5 mL minced garlic

2 Tbsp. / 30 mL olive oil

salt and black pepper to taste

$^1/_2$ cup / 125 mL salami, cut in thin strips

1 small red onion, thinly sliced

2 cups / 500 mL arugula leaves

1 cup / 250 mL shredded head lettuce

4 large round rice paper wrappers

8 thin slices provolone cheese

Place the vinegar, basil, marjoram and garlic in a mixing bowl. Drizzle in the oil, whisking constantly, until smooth and thick. Season with salt and pepper. Add the salami, red onion, arugula and lettuce to the dressing and toss well to coat.

Fill a large, shallow heat-proof dish or frying pan half-full with boiling water. Add a rice paper sheet to the water and allow to soften for about 1–2 minutes. Push any corners that curl up back down into the water. When the sheet is pliable, remove it from the water with a spatula and place it on a clean work surface.

Place two slices of provolone along the edge closest to you. Place about $^1/_4$ of the salad mixture on top of the cheese, in a row along the edge. Fold the edge of the wrapper closest to you over the salad mixture and squeeze gently to form a compact log of filling. Fold both ends of the wrapper about 1 inch / 2.5 cm over the filling to seal it in. Continue to roll the wrapper into a compact cylinder. Repeat with the remaining ingredients.

Rice Paper Rolls with Shrimp Cocktail and Mesclun

$1/4$ cup / 60 mL **ketchup**

1 Tbsp. / 15 mL **grated horseradish**

1 **lime, juice and zest**

1 cup / 250 mL **shrimp (cooked and peeled)**

3 cups / 750 mL **mesclun, washed and dried**

salt and black pepper to taste

4 large **round rice paper wrappers**

Combine the ketchup, horseradish, lime juice and zest in a mixing bowl. Add the shrimp and greens, toss well to coat and season with salt and pepper.

Fill a large, shallow heat-proof dish or frying pan half-full with boiling water. Add a rice paper sheet to the water and allow to soften, about 1–2 minutes. Push any corners that curl up back down into the water. When the sheet is pliable, remove it from the water with a spatula and place it on a clean work surface.

Place $1/4$ of the salad mixture in a row along the edge of the wrapper closest to you. Fold the edge of the wrapper closest to you over the salad mixture and squeeze gently to form a compact log of filling. Fold both ends of the wrapper about 1 inch / 2.5 cm over the filling to seal it in. Continue to roll the wrapper into a compact cylinder. Repeat with the remaining ingredients.

RICE PAPER WRAPPERS

Often used in Vietnamese and Thai cuisine, rice paper is made from a paste of rice flour and water spread thinly and dried on bamboo mats (you can still see the imprint on each sheet). They are available at Asian specialty markets. The sheets are very brittle in their dried state and become soft and pliable when soaked. Hot water quickly rehydrates the sheets (the rate of softening slows as the water cools). If you are preparing many wrappers, add fresh boiling water frequently to speed up the process. The dried sheets will keep indefinitely; store in a sealable container that protects the wrappers.